Why WITHDRAWN
Flamingos Are
Pink

Why Flamingos Are Pink

...and 250

Other Things You Should Know

Valeri R. Helterbran

TAYLOR TRADE PUBLISHING
Lanham • New York • Boulder • Toronto • Plymouth, UK

This Taylor Trade Publishing paperback edition of *Why Flamingos Are Pink* is an original publication. It is published by arrangement with the author.

Published by Taylor Trade Publishing
An imprint of The Rowman & Littlefield Publishing Group, Inc.
4501 Forbes Boulevard, Suite 200, Lanham, Maryland 20706

Estover Road, Plymouth PL6 7PY, United Kingdom

Distributed by NATIONAL BOOK NETWORK

Library of Congress Cataloging-in-Publication Data

Helterbran, Valeri R.
  Why flamingos are pink : and 250 other things you should know / Valeri R. Helterbran.—1st Taylor Trade Pub. ed.
      p.   cm.
  Includes index.
  ISBN-13: 978-1-58979-335-4 (pbk. : alk. paper)
  ISBN-10: 1-58979-335-8 (pbk. : alk. paper)
  1. Curiosities and wonders.   2. Handbooks, vade-mecums, etc.   I. Title.
  AG243.H37   2007
  031.02—dc22   2007019339

Manufactured in the United States of America.

To My Family

Buddy, Rob, and Ben
Anne and Richard Russell
All of whom have encouraged and supported my pursuits

Contents

Preface

This book was born from a love of learning and a love of teaching. Learners of all ages typically express a great interest—a sense of wonder and curiosity—in many areas of knowledge. Learning is an *infectious* condition. The more you learn, the more you want to learn! Adults, as learners themselves and as responsible parents or teachers, want to actively assist children in investigating the world around them as well as introduce new elements of wonder. All of these elements blend to create the need for a resource that can be used by learners of any age—the young, the old, and everyone in between!

Fresh topics are introduced for the readers of this book to contemplate and use as springboards for further study or contemplation. They can also be used to open doors to corollary topics or questions. While reading about a topic in this book, don't be surprised if you hear yourself exclaim, "I never knew that!" Many topics may be familiar in some ways, yet be very unfamiliar in others. This book makes the unknown, known—the perplexing, less so— and it provides grist for the mills of the brain to provide incentives to the learner to keep on learning.

Learners exhibit great curiosity in many areas and in the world around them. However, textbooks and other forums often ignore those elements of life that add texture and interest to one's general knowledge base. Often, those threads in the tapestry of learning and the depth of interest that they may inspire are lost.

The idea for this book is rooted in my widely read newspaper column, "Things Every Kid Should Know," a weekly feature in my community newspaper, the *Ligonier Echo* (Pennsylvania). Inspiration for this work is based on numerous teacher and parent requests for a book fashioned similarly to the column for use in the classroom and at home. Furthermore, since the majority of questions and topic ideas were generated by adults to meet their own learning needs, this is truly a book for learners of any age.

Each topic is introduced in the form of a question, as questions inherently invite interest. A brief response follows each question. Some topic questions are more complex than others. Follow your interests as you select questions to read; there is no set or recommended order to follow. You will notice that each topic area is appealing and that each leads to other questions or observations. You may also notice that each topic, even if unfamiliar to you, will almost without exception pop up in your life in the near future in some form or fashion. Each is likely to be related to your life in some way and is an excellent way to make connections with knowledge, experiences, or skills that you already have.

I hope that you will have fun with this book—and learn something along the way!

—Valeri R. Helterbran

Special note for teachers and parents: Learning is a wonderful way to connect with the children in your life. It can and should be a fun prospect as we are all learning beings as surely as we live and breathe! You will likely generate your own list of questions about or related to the questions presented in the book. Your children will undoubtedly do the same, and, in fact, asking them to do this may provide you with an excellent activity related to the original question.

Every attempt has been made to craft family- and school-friendly topic discussions. Be your own guide in this respect, however, and use each topic as an opportunity and as a vehicle to introduce, guide, or expand the information presented as you see fit.

Acknowledgments

No book is ever a solitary project, nor is it linear in its development. Many lifelong learners contributed topic ideas; others served as consultants for selected areas of interest; and a few stood on the sidelines lending support in various forms. Contributors are noted in the credits and resources section at the end of this work.

First and foremost, credit is due to Rick Schwab, editor of the *Ligonier Echo*. From the first moment I pitched the idea for a new weekly column called "Things Every Kid Should Know," he was unflagging in his support of the project. He instantly recognized the value and benefit of supporting the community's youth. The column, a purely voluntary contribution to the paper, paved the way for the creation of this book.

Also worthy of credit is the teaching and learning focus of my place of work, Indiana University of Pennsylvania (IUP). Founded as a normal school in 1875, IUP has never lost its teaching roots and inspiration. This is expressed in numerous ways in its support of campus faculty educative ventures such as the Center for Teaching Excellence and the Southcentral Pennsylvania Writing Project, both influential in the writing of this book.

My husband, Buddy, contributed painstaking proofreading and

suggestions throughout the process, and my children endured my seemingly endless hours on the computer!

In closing, I would also like to thank the good people at Rowman & Littlefield Publishing Group and Taylor Trade Publishing. This book would never have been possible without the encouragement, support, and hard work of Jed Lyons, Rick Rinehart, Dulcie Wilcox, and Jehanne Schweitzer.

Nature and Environment

What is a wishbone?

Furcula, taken from a Latin derivative for *fork*, is the scientific name for the bone most of us call a "wishbone." It is the forked bone in a bird's body where the two clavicles come together—what we might call a collarbone. The wishbone is perhaps most known today because of its role in family traditions at Thanksgiving. Dating back to Etruscan times, the tradition of breaking the wishbone was adopted by the Romans in 322 BC. The holder of the larger piece supposedly would be granted a wish. When the Romans conquered Britain, they brought this custom with them. Then the English, in turn, brought it with them when they colonized America. It is believed that the custom of eating turkey at Thanksgiving in America is the connection between the wishbone and the holiday. It is also believed that the practice of breaking the wishbone is the origin of phrases such as "to get a lucky break" and even "give me a break."

The bone-pulling tradition has also been nicknamed *merry*

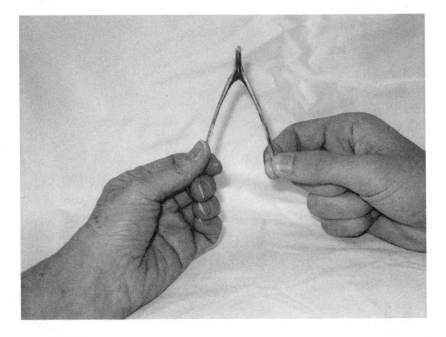

thoughts, as it has been used to "determine" the first to marry if the participants are not yet wed.

What is the purpose of an elephant's trunk?

The proboscis of an elephant serves several purposes. First and foremost, the trunk serves the same purpose as a nose. Elephants breathe through it—and can even sneeze through it just as humans do. The elephant can "sample" the air with its trunk which it then places in its mouth where certain odor-detecting organs are located. The fingerlike lip (or lips) located at the end of the trunk is very sensitive and can distinguish the texture, relative temperature, and shape of an object. It can also draw in water to drink which the elephant then squirts in its mouth, and it can grasp food items to eat, much like we use our hands. The trunk even comes in handy if an elephant is submerged in water, as it can function like a snorkel to assure an air supply. The trunk is strong enough to uproot trees, yet agile enough to pick up a seed or a coin. Elephants also use their trunks to spray themselves with water or dust. A female elephant can transport her newborn with her trunk if the need arises.

The trunk can also be used as a communication device. Elephants make noises with their trunks to greet one another or they can emit a loud, trumpeting sound. They may intertwine trunks as a greeting or use them to caress or discipline their young. The elephant can also thrash its trunk on the ground, sounding much like a sheet of metal rattling, to express displeasure or anger.

An elephant's trunk can grow up to 8 feet long and can be comprised of 60,000 muscles. Elephants are not born knowing how to fully utilize their trunks and it may take many months for mastery to occur.

What is mahimahi?

Mahimahi (*mah*-hee *mah*-hee), which means "strong strong" in Hawaiian, is a fish (*Coryphaena hippurus*). This type of fish is also called *dorado* (Spanish for golden) or dolphin fish, as they are known to swim along with dolphins. Because of this association in its name and swimming habits, many people believe incorrectly that mahimahi (a fish) *is* a dolphin (a mammal). In other words, if you were to order mahimahi from a restaurant's menu, you would not be eating Flipper!

Mahimahi (sometimes spelled with a hyphen or as one word) is a tropical, warm-water fish related to tuna. They range in size from 3 to 50 pounds and have long, deep, flat bodies. They are typically iridescent bluish green and gold with black speckling. They live only three to five years, which is unusually short for a fish of their general size. Mahimahi, due to its firm, light, and flavorful qualities, has become increasingly popular as an entrée in homes and in restaurants.

Why is it called a *field trip* when one almost never goes to see a *field*?

A field trip is generally considered a group activity or journey where individuals visit a place to observe or experience a certain phenomenon firsthand. This definition includes, but is certainly not limited to, visiting a museum, gallery, library, historic building, or a city of interest. Scientists or students of science may take a field trip to a cave, wetland area, woodland, or even a *field* (area of land) to collect specimens or data. A contemporary twist on this activity involves using the Internet to take a virtual field trip to faraway lands or other venues.

The word *field*, however, is also used in a variety of ways, such as a branch of knowledge. (One example is the field of astronomy.) It is also used to designate the observation or study of certain life forms in their natural or typical setting. For example, a professor might suggest that a doctoral student observe students in the field, which would mean observing them in a classroom setting. Therefore, the term *field trip* covers a wide variety of places or purposes which may or may not include an actual *field*.

Why and how do cats purr?

We are all familiar with the rhythmic, vibrating sound that domestic cats make when they are content. Purring is usually audible, but it can certainly be felt even if the sound is too soft to hear. Cats are also known to purr when they need or want attention, when they are in labor, when they are in pain, or when they are experiencing stressful, frightening, or traumatic circumstances. It is believed that purring during times of distress is the way that cats try to soothe themselves or relax. Kittens purr when nursing and the mother cat responds by purring, too. In this respect, purring is thought to be a form of communication.

The most widely held explanation as to how purring occurs involves an activation or stimulation of nerves in the cat's larynx (voice box). When these nerves fire, vibration of the vocal cords occurs. The act of breathing pushes air in and out, much like a bellows, influencing the cadence and volume of purring. This explanation is challenged, however, by medical research which indicates that cats can still purr even when these nerves are severed. Another possible explanation, but not as widely believed, is that purring is the result of certain vibrating blood vessels in the larynx. Purring is believed to be a voluntary act, meaning that cats purr if and when they want to purr!

What is quicksand?

Quicksand is a natural phenomenon that occurs when sand or any type of grainy soil becomes overly saturated with water. What looks like solid ground is actually a very thick "soup" of sand or soil and water. The sand particles are no longer in stable contact with each other because they are coated with a thin film of water that reduces the friction between particles and cannot bear weight. Quicksand is more likely to occur where there is an underground spring or some other water source. Locations may include beaches, riverbanks, or marshes. Most patches of quicksand are only a few inches to a few feet in depth.

Unlike what you may have seen in the movies, quicksand is not the certain killer you may think it is. It is possible to drown in quicksand, as it is possible to drown in most liquids. However, most people who get stuck survive. The key to getting unstuck from quicksand is, first and foremost, do not panic! Wildly thrashing about will cause you to become mired more quickly. The deeper you are, the more difficult it is to get out. Because your body is less dense than the mixture, however, you will have a tendency to float. Move slowly and deliberately to bring yourself to the surface. You can then work your way to solid ground or even *swim* out of any danger.

What is the difference between a donkey and a mule?

A donkey (*Equus assinus*) is a relative of the horse and is a true species. Animals that are a true species produce babies that are just like them. In other words, donkeys that breed produce baby donkeys (foals). Donkeys have noticeably long ears; a mane that is coarse, stiff, and stands upright; and a tail that somewhat resembles that of a cow. Donkeys come in many sizes—miniature, mammoth, standard, and large standard, to name a few. They can be gray, black, brown, roan, sorrel, or cream in color and may be solid or spotted. Male (jack) and female (jennet) donkeys are known for their characteristic braying (*ee*-aw *ee*-aw), although the jack is considered to be more enthusiastic in this department! Donkeys can be ridden much like horses, with a saddle or harness. They can be used to guard livestock and as companion animals for livestock and humans. They are friendly, good-natured animals; however, they tend to do what they want, not what the owner wants. Although donkeys are often called *burros* in the West, this term is considered proper when referring to midsized donkeys of wild descent.

Mules, on the other hand, are not a true species. They are equine *hybrids* that result from the breeding of a female horse and a male donkey. A similar result, although more rare, is called a "hinny." This occurs when a male horse breeds with a female donkey. As a rule, mules are sterile; they cannot produce baby mules or anything else for that matter. There *have* been a few documented exceptions to this, but this occurrence is very, very rare. Mules and hinnies (usually collectively called mules) typically show characteristics from both parents. For example, their manes are more donkeylike, whereas their tails are more horselike. Their bray is unique and usually results in a combination whinny and Aw-Aw. Mules come in most of the colors and patterns that horses and donkeys do. As with donkeys, mules can be saddled or harnessed for riding. They can carry or drag a great deal of weight and are excellent high jumpers. Intelligent animals with remarkable stamina, mules, like donkeys, are often deemed lazy or stubborn; the mule will work when the mule wants to work. Patience is a key quality for those who work with mules or donkeys.

What is a group of owls called?

Animal groups often have unusual names. A group of owls, for example, is called a "parliament" of owls. Some names seem to make sense; others are a bit of a curiosity. Group names for animals can vary with the age, gender, or stage of life of the animal involved, and for other reasons or conditions. A few examples of names of animal groups follow.

Type of Animal	Group Name
hyena	cackle or clan
bat	colony
fox	leash, skulk, or lead
buzzard	wake
porcupine	prickle
crow	murder, horde, or muster
crocodile	bask
frog	knot, army, or colony
locust	plague

For more animal group names, visit www.npwrc.usgs.gov/help/faq/animals/names.htm.

Why don't manufacturers use #1 and #2 plastic containers for all food products?

Many plastic products are marked with a number from 1 through 7. Each number represents a type of plastic that has particular qualities suitable for specific purposes. For example, PETE (polyethylene terephthalate, a #1 plastic) is typically transparent, a barrier to gas, and is heat resistant. PETE is often used for soft drinks, peanut butter, and salad dressing containers. HDPE (high density polyethylene, a #2 plastic) is inexpensive, more dense, easy to form into the desired shape, and more permeable to gas. HDPE is often used for milk, water, and juice containers.

Manufacturers choose food containers based on the qualities of the plastic and which type will best display or contain their food

product. Since some types of plastic may leach and contaminate food, manufacturers must be careful to choose the proper type to avoid harming consumers. Furthermore, different plastics have different "cleanability" capacities and when recycled, may only be suitable for certain nonfood uses.

Most communities only accept #1 and #2 plastics for recycling. According to Ellen Keefe, project director of Westmoreland (Pennsylvania) Cleanways, a nonprofit organization dedicated to keeping communities clean, the technology to recycle #1 and #2 plastics is more readily available and more economical. While the capability exists to recycle *all* numbered plastics, few communities in the United States do so.

Are all insects pests?

There are well over 1 million known species of insects. Nearly 100,000 species live in North America. Insects can be found in virtually every climate and habitat. According to the *National Audubon Field Guide to North American Insects and Spiders*, insects can be found in the air, plants, wood, soil, the bodies of other animals, and in other places. Insects are fascinating animals that exhibit an amazing degree of diversity. For example, the goliath beetle, a rain-forest insect, measures 4.5 inches long and can weigh up to 3.5 ounces. Another rain-forest insect, the rhinoceros beetle, can carry 850 times its own weight on its back; this is the same as an average-size man toting 70 or more automobiles around!

It is true that some insects cause a tremendous amount of damage to crops and trees. Some insects are even dangerous to humans. In addition, some insects are relatively harmless themselves, but carry unclean materials or deadly diseases, such as locusts, termites, fleas, mosquitoes, lice, some flies, and cockroaches. Keep in mind though that most insects serve a positive purpose, often serving as a food source for other animals, including other insects. In the United

States alone, we use in excess of 1 billion pounds of pesticides (chemicals used to kill insects and other real or perceived pests) every year. Some people choose to use more eco-friendly, organic approaches to exterminate or discourage certain insects.

Insects are typically harmless creatures and many are absolutely necessary to the survival of the planet. Insects are an important food source for humans in some parts of the world. They pollinate our plants, fertilize the soil, rid us of decaying plant and animal matter, consume other insects, and provide useful products such as honey, beeswax, and silk—and much more.

For more information on insects, visit www.bugwood.org/entomology.html.

What is the difference between a turtle, a terrapin, and a tortoise?

Turtles, terrapins, and tortoises are all reptiles and belong to the order *Testudines*. In the United States, the word "turtle" is often used interchangeably for terrapins, tortoises, and sea turtles. In fact, all of these animals *are* turtles, but they are different in several distinguishable ways. An important distinction is where these animals live. Tortoises are a land-dwelling (terrestrial) subgroup of turtles. They use water for drinking and bathing only. They have high, domed shells and have trunklike legs with stumpy, clawed feet. *Testudines* found in coastal, brackish waters are called terrapins. They are sometimes called "diamondbacks" due to the unique, angular designs on their shells. They have webbed feet with claws. Other turtles are marine or freshwater dwellers. These aquatic turtles have longer toes that are webbed or limbs that look like flippers to help with swimming, and they typically have a more flattened, streamlined shell. About 70% of all turtles live in freshwater.

A group of turtles is called a *bale*. The largest turtle living today is the leatherback. These rare sea turtles can weigh 1,500 pounds. The largest tortoise, the giant tortoise, is found on the Galapagos Islands off the coast of Ecuador. Weighing up to 500 pounds, these tortoises can live to be about 200 years old.

Why are flamingos pink?

Flamingos are beautiful, easily recognizable birds. They prefer to live in the warm, shallow, salty lagoons and lakes of Africa, Asia, Europe, and the Americas. One species, however, lives in the cold lakes of the Andes Mountains. One of the most obvious characteristics of flamingos is their reddish or pink coloration. Interestingly, many of the foods that they eat are rich in carotenoid pigment, much like the pigment in carrots. They eat shrimp and other crustaceans, algae, aquatic insects, and plankton. Without this diet, the flamingos' feathers would become grayish white. Zookeepers are careful to supplement flamingo food with special pigments to maintain their birds' beautiful color.

Flamingos have unusual, boomerang-like bills. To eat, the flamingo immerses its bill upside down in the water so that its head is actually facing backward. In that position, it uses its fleshy tongue to pump water through its bill, which acts like a strainer or filter to catch food items.

Here are a few more interesting flamingo facts:

- Flamingos live in large colonies called *pats*.
- What looks like the flamingo's knee is actually its ankle.
- Roman emperors considered flamingo tongue to be a delicacy.

What is fog?

Fog is basically a cloud that has formed at ground level. Clouds, however, are formed differently than fog. Although fog looks like smoke, it is actually made up of billions of tiny water droplets. Fog can be formed in several ways. For example, when it is cold and clear with little wind at night, the ground releases some of the heat that it absorbed during the day. As the ground cools, it subsequently cools the air near the surface to what we call the *dew point.* The dew point is the temperature at which water droplets will condense out of the air. In other words, the air is so saturated with moisture that it can no longer hold all of it. This type of ground-hugging fog is called *radiation fog.* Pilots, truck drivers, and other people who must travel in all sorts of weather use this "formula" to determine conditions. If the dew-point temperature is within 5°F (3°C) of the actual temperature, and the temperature is getting colder, the formation of fog is likely. The dew point is generally reported during most weather forecasts. Night rain can also enhance the formation of fog, but fortunately the morning sun typically evaporates or "burns it off."

Fog can also form when warm, moist air passes over colder portions of the ground especially if ice or snow is present. The cold causes the moisture in the air to condense and form fog; this is known as *advection fog.* Other types of fog include precipitation fog, upslope fog, and valley fog.

Does an ostrich really bury its head in the sand?

The ostrich (*Struthio camelus*) is the largest bird living today. Until the 1940s, this flightless bird could be found in the wild in Africa, Syria, and Saudi Arabia, but it can only be found in Central Africa now. Ostrich fossil remains, some dating back over 120 million years, have been found in Asia and Europe. An adult male (rooster) can stand from 8 to 10 feet tall and weigh from 350 to 400 pounds; the adult female (hen) is smaller. Ostriches are considered to be herbivores (plant eaters), although in the wild they have been known on occasion to also eat animal remains or insects.

Ostriches are commercially farmed in the United States and many other countries. Ostrich hide is made into fine leather and ostrich feathers are used for decoration and for cleaning materials. Ostriches are also valued for their red meat, which is often described as similar to beef, but with two-thirds less fat content.

Although they cannot fly, ostriches can run at speeds of over 40 miles per hour. Their powerful legs can deliver a formidable blow to predators. Occasionally, to avoid detection, an ostrich will lie on the ground with its neck outstretched. This behavior may have led to the belief that ostriches stick their heads in the sand when scared. In fact, they do *not* bury their heads in the sand! This is a myth. Interestingly, people often refer to this myth when speaking of someone who is in denial. For example, "Jerry is just burying his head in the sand if he thinks he can write a term paper the day before it is due."

What does Indian summer mean?

Indian summer is a period of unusually warm and dry weather with light or calm winds that occurs in autumn. Although the term is often applied to any period of warm autumnal weather, by definition a true Indian summer follows a killing freeze or frost. Autumn may host several Indian summers or none at all. Periods of Indian summer may last from a few days to more than a week.

The origin of the term is undetermined. One theory is that North American Native Americans would use these periods of warm weather to harvest late crops and to prepare for the winter months ahead. Some speculate that this time was a favored hunting season. Other sources cite the custom of early English-speaking settlers to use the word "Indian" for things that were similar to familiar items or for things not true or that were an imitation—hence, an Indian summer was a false summer.

The first known usage of the term was by French-American farmer St. John de Crèvecoeur, in a letter dated January 17, 1778. Indian summer is a term typically used (although certainly not exclusively) in the middle-Atlantic and New England states. It is occasionally called "goose summer," and in England, "Saint Martin's summer." Interestingly, the term "Indian summer" is also sometimes used quite differently to describe success found late in life!

What is the *eye* of a hurricane?

A hurricane is a powerful tropical weather system with a well-defined circulation pattern that has developed a constant wind speed of 74 miles per hour or more. Hurricanes can range in size from 300 to 500 miles in diameter. It is believed that the term "hurricane" comes from the Mayan storm god, Hunraken, or perhaps, Huracan, a god considered evil by the Taino people of the Caribbean.

Hurricanes have an "eye." This is located at or near the center of the storm and is an area of relative calm with a warmer temperature, light winds, little or no precipitation, and fair skies. The eye typically measures 20 to 30 miles wide. The top of the eye may be 50,000 feet above ground. However, the eye is bound by the eye wall, a ring of thunderstorms with dramatic updrafts and downdrafts that produce some of the most violent weather associated with the hurricane. More intense hurricanes may have concentric eye walls which help maintain the storm's structure and intensity.

Hurricane damage is typically caused by high winds, torrential rain, storm surge, and/or flooding. Tornadoes and severe thunderstorms are often spawned from hurricanes, causing additional hazards. Billions of dollars in property damage and loss of life can result if the storm reaches land. Approximately 100 tropical disturbances occur in the Atlantic Ocean every year between May and November. Of these, six become hurricanes, with an average of two making landfall in the United States. Fortunately, improvements in weather predicting have enabled us to better prepare for these weather events.

Can humans live on Mars?

Mars, the "Red Planet," is named for Mars, the Roman god of war, and has historically been a topic of great speculation, fantasy, and interest. It is easy to see how fictional visions of Martians have endured as Mars and earth do share certain similarities. For starters, Mars has two polar caps, a day of 24.6 hours, an atmosphere of gases that includes some oxygen and water vapor, an equatorial temperature at or near 72°F in the summer, distinct seasons, and certain terrain (volcanoes and canyons, for example) resembling, in some ways, that of earth.

However, the differences in the two planets far outweigh these similar characteristics when considering the possibility of humans living on Mars. Scientists believe that Mars may have once been a warm, watery, earth-like planet. Fossil evidence suggesting microscopic life has been found in a Martian meteorite, but scientists debate whether or not clear proof exists. A vast, frozen desert in large measure, Mars' average temperature is about −67°F, but ranges from below −194°F to the aforementioned 72°F. No surface water is present on Mars. Although NASA reports evidence that suggests that a small amount of liquid water *may* exist on Mars, scientists also hotly debate this issue! Mars has a thin atmosphere composed of about 95% carbon dioxide (the waste gas that we exhale) and has no ozone layer to filter out damaging ultraviolet light from the sun. In addition, the weather includes blinding storms of rust-colored (iron oxide) dust with gusts up to 100 miles per hour. For these reasons alone, it is plain to see that dramatic accommodations would need to be made for human beings to actually live on Mars!

What is brackish water?

Brackish water results from the natural mixing of seawater (salt) and freshwater where these types of water bodies meet. When this occurs, one resulting habitat is called an estuary. Estuaries are vitally important to us as they serve as an environment for many living things to breed, be sheltered, or to live out their lives. Brackish water can also be found in some aquifers, according to certain fossil deposits.

Estuary areas provide us with recreational opportunities, food, and other products. Brackish water is generally undrinkable, but if its salt content (salinity) is low enough, some communities are able to purify it. The saline content typically varies in brackish water depending on the amount of freshwater and saltwater mixing and the rate of evaporation. Plants and animals that live in brackish water must be highly adaptable to survive.

The largest brackish estuary in the United States is the watershed of the Chesapeake Bay. Thanks to agreements between Pennsylvania, Maryland, and Virginia, this estuary is healthier due to tighter regulations on sewage treatment, chemical and industrial waste disposal, and other sources of pollution. Pennsylvania plays an important role in this as the Susquehanna River is the Chesapeake Bay's largest tributary and provides it with 90% of the freshwater that empties into it. It is the freshwater from Pennsylvania that mixes with the saltwater to make brackish water farther downstream. According to the Pennsylvania Department of Conservation and Natural Resources (DCNR), true brackish water reaches into Pennsylvania from the Delaware Bay, creating a small estuary.

The term *brackish* is also used to describe something that is unpleasant, spoiled, or distasteful. Some examples of this usage are:

- ❧ My poor judgment had a brackish effect on my relationship with others.
- ❧ From Lance Armstrong in *It's Not about the Bike*, "I gagged, and tasted something metallic and brackish in the back of my throat."

Why do camels have a hump?

Camels have several important physical features that help them adapt to their desert environment. To protect them from sand, particularly during sandstorms, they have long eyelashes to protect their eyes and nostrils that flatten to keep sand out of the nose. Their feet are broad and have padded toes to help them walk on the sand. Among other adaptations, camels have a hump on their back. Contrary to what many believe, this structure is made of fatty tissue, not stored water. Its size varies depending on the available food supply and the type of work a camel does. A camel's hump can weigh up to 80 pounds! It provides sustenance for the camel when the food supply is poor. This is especially important for living in the desert where food and water can be sparse. Camels can go for days without food or water. In fact, as the camel's body uses the sustenance in its hump, the hump shrinks and can even sag, hanging at the camel's side. The hump will return to its normal state with proper food and rest.

There are two types of camel. The dromedary has two humps and the Bactrian has one. Adult camels weigh between 700 and 1,500 pounds and can live about 50 years.

Where does cork come from?

Cork is actually the bark of a certain tree, the cork oak (*Quercus suber*). The cork oak grows in the Mediterranean Sea region, primarily in Portugal, Spain, Algeria, Tunisia, Morocco, Italy, and France. Portugal alone produces over 50% of the cork we use in the United States. For optimal growth, the cork oak requires plenty of sun and a combination of low amounts of rainfall and high humidity. The formation of cork bark is nature's way of providing the tree protection from temperature extremes, insects, fire, and other threats.

Strict laws govern the harvesting of cork in order to protect the trees themselves and to assure a stable crop of high-quality cork. During the summer months, highly skilled laborers use a special axe to strip the cork bark from the trees making sure that no more than one-third of the bark is stripped away at any one time. They also take care to avoid damaging the cambium, the delicate layer of the tree that forms the cork bark itself. Stripping the bark does not harm the tree. Cork oak trees are typically first harvested at the age of 25 and can be harvested no sooner than every nine years thereafter for the tree's expected 150- to 250-year lifespan. Processing the bark results in virtually no waste. There is a use for every little scrap of cork.

What is mushroom soil?

Mushroom soil (also called *mushroom earth, compost,* or *substrate*) is typically made by commercial mushroom growers. According to the American Mushroom Institute, mushrooms are grown on a special compost mixture of wheat straw (often horse bedding straw), hay, corncobs, cotton seed hulls, gypsum, and chicken manure. Some mushroom growers alter this "recipe" to include rye straw, grape crushings, soybean meal, and/or other "ingredients." Commercial growers are quite precise in adhering to their preferred compost mixture. A layer of peat moss and limestone is typically added on the top of the compost mixture; it is here that the mushrooms grow. After the mushrooms have been grown and harvested, the remaining compost mixture is steam pasteurized to kill any insects or weed seeds and, being of no further use to the grower, it is packaged for sale. Among other places, landscape and garden centers offer this product for use in home gardens. Most gardeners add mushroom soil to the existing soil in their gardens or use it as mulch. Gardeners and farmers prize mushroom soil because of its rich, slowly released nutrients and water-holding ability.

Because it is so concentrated, it is not advised to plant directly into fresh mushroom soil.

Pennsylvania is the largest producer of mushrooms in the United States, followed by California. In fact, Kennett Square, Pennsylvania (Chester County), claims to be the mushroom capital of the world. Pennsylvania grows about 50% of the mushrooms consumed in America, primarily the common white button mushroom (*Agaricus bisporus*).

What is dry ice?

Dry ice is *frozen* carbon dioxide (CO_2), plain and simple! Carbon dioxide is the waste gas that we exhale when we breathe. It is also the gas that puts the bubbly zip in carbonated soft drinks. Dry ice is an extremely cold substance. Its surface temperature is $-109.3°F$ ($-78.5°C$). Because of this, it is used commercially to freeze or refrigerate food or other items in storage or during transportation. Among other things, dry ice is also used in school science experiments, to make "fog" for theatrical purposes, and for special effects in punch bowls or other beverages.

An interesting fact about dry ice, a solid, is that it has no liquid state. Dry ice changes directly into its gaseous state when exposed to water or air. This phenomenon is known as "sublimation." There is no "watery" stage as when an ice cube melts, hence the name "dry." Dry ice can be stored in an ice chest or other insulated container to slow the sublimation process.

Although dry ice is considered nontoxic, special precautions must be observed in handling or using it. These include, but are not limited to, avoiding all direct skin contact, using insulated gloves, and never eating dry ice. In addition, respiratory difficulties may result if dry ice "fog" is directly inhaled, especially if it is concentrated or when in an enclosed environment. Never add water to dry ice for use in a closed container. This accelerates sublimation, which may result in the explosion of the container (and injury to you!). Also, if used in direct contact with food or beverages, care should be taken to use "food grade" dry ice to assure that no undesirable contaminants are present.

To learn more about dry ice, visit www.dryiceinfo.com.

What is a shooting star?

For starters, a shooting star, sometimes called a *falling star*, is not a star at all; it is a meteor. According to NASA (www.nasa.gov), meteors originate from a number of sources. One meteor source is a comet. A comet is a frozen mass of rocks, dust, and gases—something like a big, dirty snowball or iceberg. Throughout its travels in space, the comet begins to melt, which frees rocks and dust particles. Called *meteoroids*, these freed bodies are on their own to travel in space. Scientists estimate that billions of meteoroids enter the earth's atmosphere on a daily basis. Once they enter the atmosphere, they are called *meteors*. Most meteors are no bigger than a speck of dust or a grain of sand. Others are quite large. As they typically travel at a speed faster than the space shuttle, enough friction is created to make the meteor glow; most burn up completely. What can be seen from earth for a few fleeting seconds is what we call a shooting star, the glowing phase of the meteor that occurs about 50 to 68 miles above the earth's surface.

Although they are unpredictable in occurrence, shooting stars can be observed nightly. All you need is patience and a clear sky. Large meteors, more rare, may weigh tons and create a much larger and longer glow called a *fireball*. Additionally, several times every year in a largely predictable fashion, earth's orbit coincides with the path of a comet and its trail of debris as it orbits the sun. When this occurs, the event is called a *meteor shower* and viewers may be treated to tens, hundreds, or perhaps thousands of shooting stars.

Although our atmosphere provides excellent protection, some meteors survive their blazing trip and impact earth. Now called *meteorites*, most at this point are so small that they cause no damage. Most meteorites of recoverable size result from fireballs. Of the 150 impacts studied on earth, a well-known meteorite crash site is Barringer's Crater, located near Winslow, Arizona, the result of a meteorite crash at least 50,000 years ago. Another impact occurred in 1908 in the remote region of the Tunguska Basin in Siberia. This event generated enough heat and damage to destroy 770 square miles of forestland. Evidence of the destruction is still visible today.

What is all of that red skin on a turkey's head called?

The turkey does indeed have unique structures on its head. The head and neck area of the turkey have no feathers. The color of the skin ranges from white to gray, bluish white, blue, pink, and red. One of the most obvious features on the head is the snood or dew bill, the elongated, fingerlike appendage that grows from the base of the top of the bill (the beak) and hangs down the side of the turkey's face. Bright pinkish red fleshy bumps called *carnucles* cover the head and neck area; some may be droopy, others may be wart-like. A third structure is called the *wattle* or *dewlap*. This is the baggy, loose skin on the turkey's throat.

Although both the male (called a tom or gobbler) and the female (hen) turkeys have these structures, they are considerably more pronounced on the male, becoming particularly red and prominent when he is trying to impress the ladies. During courtship, he will also gobble robustly, strut vigorously, puff his body feathers, drag his wings, and spread his tail feathers into a magnificent fan.

Why is summer warmer than winter?

Many people believe erroneously that our seasons are caused by the varying distances of the earth from the sun as it travels on its elliptical orbit around the sun. Not so! Interestingly, the Northern Hemisphere is actually *closer* to the sun during the winter months. Our seasons are caused by the tilt of the earth (23.5°) on its imaginary axis. During the summer months, the Northern Hemisphere is tilted more toward the sun. The rays of the sun hit the earth at a more direct angle than in the winter when the tilt is away from the sun. Furthermore, being tilted toward the sun increases the length of time the sun remains above the horizon. More sun time plus the more direct angle equals warmer weather.

Another common misperception is that the earth tips and sways on its axis as it orbits around the sun. This, too, is not so. The earth largely remains tilted in the *same* direction during the entire year-long orbit. It is the earth's position relative to the sun that accounts for our seasons.

While the Northern Hemisphere experiences the warmth of summer, it is wintertime in the Southern Hemisphere, in for example, South America and Australia.

Source: http://csep10.phys.utk.edu/astr161/lect/index.html.

What is a tsunami?

A tsunami (soo-*nahm*-ee) is a series of waves caused by an underwater landslide, earthquake, or volcanic eruption. Its name is taken from the Japanese word for "harbor wave." In the open ocean, these waves can travel more than 450 miles per hour, yet may be difficult to detect at the surface by the naked eye. They typically radiate outward from the source of the disturbance, much like the ripples that are formed when one tosses a pebble into water. If these waves get close to the shore, their speed decreases and their height increases before they crash onto the land. These waves can range between 10 feet to 100 feet in height. In the United States, Tsunami Warning Centers in Hawaii and Alaska monitor tsunami-causing occurrences, track tsunamis, and issue warnings when warranted.

Often mistakenly called "tidal waves," tsunamis have caused billions of dollars in property damage as well as the loss of many lives worldwide. According to the United States Geological Survey (USGS), the great Indian Ocean tsunami of 2004 was the deadliest in recorded history. Affecting 11 countries, it released the energy of 23,000 atomic bombs (Hiroshima-type) and at day's end, more than 150,000 people were dead or missing; millions of others were homeless.

Sources: http://www.fema.gov/rrr/talkdiz/tsunami.shtm; http://www.usgs.gov.

How do bees make honey?

Honeybees are important insects. They produce honey and pollinate many of the plant foods that we eat. Their biological name, *Apis mellifera*, means "honey carrier." This name, technically, is not accurate as it is actually nectar, the sweet fluid produced by flowers, that is carried back to the hive to make honey. After worker bees (all female) gather the nectar, they store it in a stomachlike structure called a "honey sac" where it is mixed with enzymes. Back at the hive, these bees empty the nectar in the sac into a wax cell or pass it to a "house" worker bee to deposit it. The cells are left open and fanned by bee wings until enough evaporation occurs for the nectar mixture to become honey. The cell is then sealed with beeswax. Honeybees make honey to use as food during the long winter months when flower nectar is not available. A grouping of these wax cells is called a honeycomb.

The average worker bee generates about one-twelfth of a teaspoon of honey during her lifetime. The color and flavor of the honey results from the types of flowers visited by the bees. Fortunately, man-made honeybee hives can produce 20 pounds of excess honey (depending on the size), which is then harvested by the commercial or hobbyist beekeeper. It is estimated that there are 211,600 beekeepers in the United States alone.

The average adult American consumes approximately one pound of honey per year, the product of two million bee visits to flowers. It is recommended, however, that babies under the age of 12 months *not* eat honey as spores causing a certain type of botulism may be present. Honeybees themselves are usually not a threat to humans, despite our concern about being stung. Honeybees will only sting when they are taunted, frightened, or otherwise threatened.

For more information, visit www.honey.com and read *The Honey Files: A Bee's Life* by the National Honey Board.

Why is the Dead Sea considered dead?

Interestingly, the Dead Sea is actually a saltwater lake. Forming part of the border between Jordan and Israel, it is positioned at the mouth of the Jordan River and, covering about 400 square miles, measures approximately 11 miles by 50 miles at its widest and longest points. The Dead Sea is the saltiest body of water in the world (seven to nine times saltier than ocean water) and it is also the lowest place (about 1,312 feet below sea level) on earth's surface. The water is so salty, no fish can live in it. Only a few plants and brine shrimp can survive there, hence the name "Dead." The saltiness allows swimmers to float without difficulty, but when they leave the water, they typically sport a salty crust on their skin.

The Dead Sea is an active tourist area as its warm mineral-laden water and mud reputedly have therapeutic and restorative powers. The salty waters are also used to produce various medicines, table salt, and fertilizer.

Called the Salt Sea in the Bible, the Dead Sea is particularly known as the approximate location of the infamous cities of Sodom and Gomorrah, now believed to be under the water at the southern end of the sea. In addition, in 1947, shepherds discovered numerous documents in caves near the sea. Referred to as the Dead Sea Scrolls, these precious manuscripts include all of the books of the Old Testament (minus Esther) and other writings.

Is there a difference between a bison and a buffalo?

Scientifically, what many people call the American buffalo (*Bison bison*) is not really a buffalo at all; it is a bison. Bison are not related to true buffalo (Asia's water buffalo and Africa's Cape buffalo) and are only distantly related to the wisent, a European buffalo. Bison are actually more closely related to the cow. However, the common interchangeable use of *buffalo* and *bison* has made the terms virtually synonymous, albeit incorrect.

Sixty million bison once roamed the central plains from Mexico to Canada. By the late 19th century, the numbers had dwindled to fewer that a thousand due in large measure to unregulated hunting of the animals by settlers and explorers. Alarmed at the prospect of the bison's imminent extinction, zoologist William T. Hornaday

initiated efforts to save this magnificent and unique symbol of America. Today, over 350,000 bison roam public and private lands in North America.

The American bison is the largest land mammal living on the continent since the Ice Age. A mature bull bison can weigh 2,000 pounds or more; a mature female bison can weigh from 900 to 1,100 pounds. The average life span of the bison ranges from 20 to 25 years, although living to 30 or more years of age is not unheard of. Males and females have permanent horns made of hairlike material and can run up to 30 to 35 miles per hour.

Yellowstone National Park is home to approximately 3,500 bison, the nation's largest public herd; numerous private herds are located throughout the country. Bison are wild animals and contact with them should be avoided except by experienced handlers.

What is known about the eastern woodlands bison?

Years ago, Pennsylvania was inhabited by a species of bison (*Bison bison pennsylvanicus*) called the eastern woodlands bison. It is described as having a darker color, longer legs, a bigger chest, a smaller pelvis and shoulder "hump," and a shorter tail than the familiar plains or American bison. What little we know today about this now-extinct species is due to the research of author and naturalist Glover M. Allen (1879–1942), and the works of Henry W. Shoemaker (1882–1958), an authority on Pennsylvania history, folklore, and wildlife. Shoemaker traveled extensively in Pennsylvania and surrounding areas to document the knowledge and accounts of community elders. Accuracy may not be absolute since many findings are based more on local tradition than on documented fact. Among numerous titles published by Shoemaker, *A Pennsylvania Bison Hunt* (1915) is considered to be a blend of lore, legend, and history. It chronicles formidable bison interactions with humans on the Pennsylvania frontier and the demise of this species of bison, primarily at the hand of settlers and explorers.

According to Glover M. Allen, the probable range of the eastern woodlands bison extended from western New York through the mountains of Pennsylvania, West Virginia, and Tennessee, and into Georgia. The last known herd in Pennsylvania was reportedly killed during the winter of 1799–1800 in the White Mountains of Union County, with several individual bison surviving for a few more years. The last known eastern woodlands bison was killed in 1825 in Valley Head, West Virginia.

To read more about bison, see Glover M. Allen's book, *Extinct and Vanishing Mammals of the Western Hemisphere.*

What is heat lightning?

Heat lightning is a lay term given to faint flashes of light seen from the lightning of distant thunderstorms—storms that are too far away for the thunder to be heard. If conditions are favorable, this lightning may be seen at distances of up to 100 miles away! What the observer actually sees is the diffused reflection of the light from the lightning on clouds or other particles in the air. The origin of the term *heat lightning* probably came from the witnessing of this phenomenon on warm summer evenings.

Why do we have standard and daylight saving time?

Until the late 19th century, the determination of time was largely a local matter. In 1883 the railroads in the United States and Canada attempted to standardize time in order to lessen confusion with their rail schedules. Following suit in 1918, the United States Congress adopted standard time zones based on the ideas proposed by the railroads.

Although Benjamin Franklin originally suggested the idea of daylight saving in 1784, William Willett, an English builder, is widely credited for originating "summer time" in 1916, what Americans refer to as daylight saving time (DST). The United States instituted DST during World War I and World War II in order to save fuel needed for the war effort, and during the 1973 Arab oil embargo due to fuel shortages. Other than these occasions, Americans used DST sporadically based on local laws and customs. As this caused confusion and frustration in traveling, broadcasting, and communication, the Uniform Time Act of 1966 established a uniform system of DST (within each time zone) throughout the United States. Unless in a time of national crisis, individual states could choose to use DST or not, but any state opting to use DST was required to use the uniform system. We continue to use DST today to save fuel and to accommodate a majority of Americans who enjoy an extra hour of daylight during the warmer months. DST in the United States begins at 2 a.m. on the second Sunday in March and ends at the same time on the first Sunday in November.

DST is not observed in Hawaii, the eastern time zone of Indiana, and Arizona (with the exception of the Navajo Indian Reservation). Approximately 70 countries worldwide use some form of DST.

To learn more about daylight saving time, visit http://webexhib its.org/daylightsaving.

Why do we switch to daylight saving time at 2 a.m.?

Daylight saving time (DST) in the United States begins at 2 a.m. (local time) on the second Sunday in March. Two o'clock in the

morning was chosen because it seemed practical to minimize disruptions to people's schedules, in particular, public transportation schedules, those on early shift, and those wishing to attend church services. Changing the time at this hour also minimally affected restaurants as many states prohibit the sale of alcohol beyond 2 a.m.

Two o'clock is also a favored time in the fall to return to standard time for many of the reasons noted above and in order to prevent having the first day of standard time revert to the day before because of turning the clocks back an hour.

What is a blue moon?

Blue moon is a term used to describe the phenomenon of two full moons occurring during the same calendar month, the second of which is called a "blue moon." The current use of this astronomical term originated in 1946. The average period of time between two full moons is 29.5 days; the length of the average month is 30.5 days. Therefore, the occurrence of a blue moon is a rarity—approximately one every two and a half years. In daily usage, the phrase "once in a blue moon" is used to mean rarely, infrequently, not often, or to describe an unusual event.

The color of the moon does not turn blue during a blue moon. However, there are times when the moon may appear bluish in color. This is typically caused by the dust and smoke generated from significant volcanic eruptions or major forest fires that rise high into the earth's atmosphere.

Native Americans in pre-Colonial times gave full moons distinctive or unusual names to help keep track of the seasons. Some of these names were adopted by the settlers, who also added a few of their own. Examples of full moon names include, Wolf Moon, Snow Moon, Worm or Lenten Moon, Flower Moon, Buck Moon,

Harvest Moon, and Hunter's Moon. Some of these names are still used today.

To learn more about blue moons, visit www.obliquity.com/astro/bluemoon.html.

What is a cria?

Cria is the term for a baby llama or a baby alpaca. Many animal offspring are called by unusual or unfamiliar names. Here are some examples:

bat: pup	kangaroo: joey
eel: elver	oyster: spat
fish (generally): fry	rooster: cockerel
giraffe: calf	skunk: kit
grouse: cheeper	swan: cygnet

Do honeybees die after they sting someone?

Honeybees (*Apis mellifera*) have barbed stingers. When they sting a human, they are unable to easily pull away due to the relative elasticity of human skin. In essence, they become stuck. At that point, the bee is either swatted to death or pulls hard enough to tear out the lower end of its abdomen (a fatal injury) to escape. Because of this, honeybees typically can only sting once. (On the other hand, wasps, hornets, and yellow jackets have smooth, lancelike stingers. They can sting multiple people multiple times.)

Because the honeybee's venom sac remains attached to the stinger after stinging, it is important to remove the stinger as quickly as possible. Otherwise, the gland continues to pump the venom into the victim of the sting for several minutes after the bee has flown away to die. Conventional advice tells us to scrape or flick the stinger away with a fingernail, credit card, or the like. Using tweezers or otherwise pinching the stinger away tends to squeeze more venom into the person stung. However, recent research suggests that *speed* in removal of the stinger is more important than the *method* used to remove it.

Bees, wasps, bumblebees, hornets, and other stinging insects are usually not aggressive. They react to what they perceive to be a danger or a threat and sting to protect themselves or their colonies. Stings typically cause pain, swelling, redness, and itching. Treatment for most bee stings may include washing the area and applying ice, meat tenderizer, or other topical treatments to lessen the discomfort. Some people, however, have severe reactions to bee stings, including severe swelling, fainting, or breathing difficulties. Medical attention should be sought immediately if these symptoms occur.

Why do cats love catnip?

Catnip is a perennial herb of the mint family (*Nepeta cataria*). The active ingredient in this herb is nepetalactone. When cats encounter catnip, about two-thirds of them experience an intense reaction characterized by licking, biting, rubbing, or rolling in it; losing interest in anything else; and, in general, just behaving in a somewhat euphoric fashion. Other cats (and animals of other species) are seemingly unaffected by catnip, prompting scientists to believe the reaction to catnip is genetic. Male and female cats react to catnip equally, as do cats of different breeds. The catnip "experience" lasts only a few minutes even if the catnip remains in the vicinity. Exposure to catnip appears to be harmless and nonaddictive to cats. Cats prefer fresh catnip. Because the potency of catnip diminishes rather quickly, many cat lovers store catnip in the freezer.

Native to Europe and Asia, catnip is now found growing wild in North America and can be easily cultivated in home gardens. Catnip has been used historically for cooking, medicinal purposes, and as an insect repellent.

Does the burning of leaves pollute the air?

Simply put, yes. Burning leaves in the autumn was a typical activity nationwide in North America until recently. Now, many municipalities discourage this practice or ban it outright. Leaves are typically moisture rich, and when burned produce a great deal of airborne particulate matter in the form of smoke. Particulates initiate or aggravate respiratory conditions resulting in irritated eye, nose, and throat membranes. In addition, coughing, chest pain, wheezing, difficulty breathing, and other symptoms may occur. Carbon monoxide, hydrocarbons, and other chemicals associated with certain cancers and other diseases are also found in the smoke of burning leaves. Particles from leaf burning can remain lodged in the lungs for months—or longer. These factors are especially dire for those suffering from asthma or heart or lung conditions. In addition, leaf burning is often cited as the initial cause for home and forest fires.

Because local governments also often prohibit leaf disposal in landfills, they may offer leaf disposal or collection options. If such means are not available, composting is considered to be a safe, eco-friendly alternative to burning, as is using fallen leaves to mulch garden areas.

2

The Human Body

hat is leprosy?

Leprosy is an infectious disease which attacks the skin, mucous membranes, eyes, and peripheral nerves (nerves outside of the central nervous system). In cases that go untreated, permanent disfigurement, muscle paralysis of the hands and feet, and/or blindness are likely. An obvious symptom of leprosy involves the skin. The disease is characterized by multiple lesions—patches of lighter-colored skin that are typically thickened and deadened to sensation. Often large, cosmetically disfiguring growths or nodules occur.

Leprosy is caused by *Mycobacterium leprae*. This bacterium was discovered by G. A. Hansen in 1873, so leprosy is also called Hansen's disease. Researchers suspect that this disease is spread from person to person via respiratory droplets. Fortunately, it appears to be relatively difficult to transmit. Historically, individuals who exhibited symptoms of leprosy were despised as they were thought to be unclean, cursed, or being punished for bad acts. Victims were often ostracized and isolated in what were called "leper colonies" until they succumbed to the disease.

Today, there are about 300,000 cases of leprosy diagnosed each year—approximately 100 of those in the United States. Most of the cases are found in Africa, Brazil, Madagascar, India, and Nepal. With dramatic improvements in medical science, the diagnosis and treatment of leprosy are now relatively easy and the World Health Organization (WHO) offers free treatment to anyone affected. However, timely recognition and treatment are critical factors in avoiding permanent disabilities and disfigurement.

Why do people hiccup?

Everybody hiccups from time to time—even babies before they are born. Other mammals hiccup, too. The cause of hiccuping is varied and ranges from eating too much too fast, swallowing too much air, inhaling anesthesia during surgery, exposure to cold air or cold water, or stress. All of us have a dome-shaped muscle at the base of our chest called the diaphragm. It works by pulling down when we inhale to help draw air into our lungs. It pushes upward to assist in the process of exhaling. When any of the circumstances noted above occur, the vagus nerve may become stimulated, which causes the diaphragm to lower quickly. The intake of breath is halted by the closure of the glottis (space between the vocal cords), which produces the *hic* sound of hiccups.

Hiccups can last for a few minutes to days to weeks. The longest bout of hiccuping was documented in a farmer whose hiccups extended from 1922 to 1987. Long periods of hiccuping may be caused by more serious medical problems and should be reported to a health-care professional. People have used a variety of home remedies to cure hiccups, some more effective than others. In time, hiccups will cease on their own.

Why does skin wrinkle when exposed to water for a long period of time?

Think of what your fingertips or the bottoms of your feet look like after you have been in a swimming pool or bathtub for an extended period of time. Skin in these areas is thicker, which is helpful in protecting us from daily wear and tear. These areas get wrinkly or pruney in appearance after soaking in water because the outer layers of skin (dead keratin cells) absorb water. When this occurs, the skin expands. Naturally, your fingertips and the soles of your feet themselves do not expand, so the skin has no other option than to wrinkle somewhat. After getting out of the water, the excess water evaporates from the outer layers of the skin and the skin returns to its normal appearance.

What is a goose bump?

Skin has many protective features. Among these are hair erector muscles. Small muscles are attached to hairs on the body. When we become cold, the muscles contract, which raises the hairs and the surrounding skin. Our skin becomes bumpy-looking and that is what we call having goose bumps, goose pimples, or gooseflesh. Scientists believe that in our distant past we had much more hair on our bodies than we do now. When goose bumps occurred, many hairs were raised; air was trapped under the hair providing warmth due to the extra insulation. This biological response is exhibited by hairy animals. It protects them against the elements.

We can also get goose bumps when we are scared, threatened, or stimulated in some way. Here again, we see this response in certain animals. When an animal is threatened, goose bumps occur, causing its hair to stand up. This makes the animal look bigger and more impressive to its foes. Visualize what the hair (fur) looks like on a cat and a dog when they first meet!

Who was Robert Pershing Wadlow?

Robert Pershing Wadlow (1918–1940) was the tallest man in documented medical history (at least since Biblical times). He was born and raised in Alton, Illinois. He grew to 8 feet, 11.1 inches in height and weighed 490 pounds at his death. He had a condition called gigantism, the result of a highly overactive pituitary gland. The pituitary is a small gland located at the base of the brain which produces growth hormone. Wadlow caused quite a sensation in his day and toured for a while with the Ringling Brothers Circus. He also achieved great fame as a result of his promotional work for the International Shoe Company. He wore a size 38 shoe! His great height necessitated leg braces to help him walk. He is said to have had very little feeling in his feet and lower legs. The braces often caused blisters, without him being aware of it. One blister became infected and led to his death.

Wadlow was well liked and considered an inspirational figure. He was a Boy Scout and a high school graduate, and he attended college. In 1985 he was immortalized when the citizenry of his hometown erected a bronze statue of him in his memory.

What is a southpaw?

A southpaw is someone who writes with or otherwise predominantly uses his or her left hand for tasks. The origination of this term is credited to Finley Peter Dunne, sportswriter and humorist, in the late 1880s. Baseball diamonds of that day were typically designed with home plate situated to the west in line with the setting sun. A left-handed pitcher threw the ball with his left hand (paw) which would be on the *southern* side of the diamond. The term *southpaw* caught on in baseball, then in other sports such as boxing, and then applied to lefties in general.

About 13% of the world's population is left-handed. Several notable lefties include Alexander the Great, Bill Gates, Bill Clinton, Paul McCartney, Jerry Seinfeld, Babe Ruth, Prince William, Henry Ford, and Leonardo da Vinci.

What is a wart?

A wart is a benign (noncancerous) skin growth caused by a certain virus called a human papillomavirus (HPV). The virus causes skin cells to overmultiply in a spot or spots. They are usually the color of the skin and feel rough. Other types of warts can be dark, flat, and/or smooth. HPV enters the body through broken skin, for example, from the biting of fingernails, picking hangnails, or scuffing feet. Damaged skin gives the virus an opportunity to enter the body.

According to the American Academy of Dermatology (www.aad.org), the most typical type of wart is the common or seed wart. These tend to grow on the fingers, around the nails, or on the backs of one's hands. Plantar warts affect the soles of the feet. They may grow in clusters called mosaic warts. Plantar warts are often painful because walking on them forces the growth back into the skin. Flat warts are usually small, smooth warts. They may appear in rather large numbers (20 to 100), commonly on the face or legs.

Warts are contagious. However, some people tend to get warts; others do not seem to be affected. Warts will often disappear on their own, especially in children. Various treatments can be used to get rid of warts. Although over-the-counter methods are available, it is best to consult your physician to make sure that the growth is indeed a wart. Medical professionals use a variety of treatments including chemical remedies, laser therapies, cryotherapy (freezing), or surgical methods to remove warts.

How did eyeteeth get their name?

Humans have four eyeteeth, two upper and two lower. They are located close to the front of the jaw and have a pointy appearance. Think about Bram Stoker's fictional character, Count Dracula; his "fangs" are greatly enlarged eyeteeth.

Eyeteeth are called *cuspids* (the correct dental term), *dog teeth*, or *canines*. Shakespeare's *The Winter's Tale* refers to the eyetooth as a "pugging tooth." In many carnivorous mammals, these teeth serve the purpose of grasping or tearing food. The size of cuspids varies from species to species, and they may be small or absent in herbivorous mammals.

The naming of eyeteeth is simple enough. The upper cuspids are located in a direct line under one's eyes. The lower cuspids were formerly nicknamed the "stomach teeth" for the corresponding reason, but in today's usage, all four are called eyeteeth.

Who was Karl Landsteiner?

Although everyone's blood may look the same, there are distinct and important differences. An Austrian scientist and medical doctor named Karl Landsteiner (1868–1943) was the first to classify blood according to the differences that he noted. His work earned him the Nobel Prize for Physiology/Medicine in 1930 for his discoveries.

Landsteiner classified blood into the now recognized A, B, AB, and O blood types. Type O is the most common blood type in the United States, exhibited by approximately 46% of the population. About 40% have type A, followed by 10% with type B and only 4% having type AB. Interestingly, type A is the most common blood type in Japan, Australia, the Scandinavian countries, and in Native Americans.

If you are:	You can donate blood to:	You can receive blood from:
Type O	A, B, AB, O	O
Type A	A, AB	O, A
Type B	B, AB	O, B
Type AB	AB	A, B, O, AB

Individuals with type O blood are considered to be universal donors as their blood can be given to anyone. Those with type AB are considered to be universal receivers because they can receive any type of blood. Blood transfusions are complicated by something called the Rh factor. To assure a safe process, after blood is donated, it is checked for type and Rh factor and is screened for certain diseases.

Essentially, Landsteiner found that some blood had a chemical molecule which he called molecule "A" (type A), others had a different molecule which he called molecule "B" (type B), while still others had both molecules (type AB). The blood of many individuals had neither molecule (type O). His work led to our understanding that blood is not all the same. Mixing different types of blood may cause blood to clump or stick together (agglutinate), which can lead to serious physical complications or death. Therefore, it is important for all individuals to know their own blood type and the blood type of their loved ones.

What is diabetes?

According to the American Diabetes Association, "diabetes is a disease in which the body does not produce or properly use insulin. Insulin, made in the pancreas, is the hormone that is needed to convert sugar, starches, and other food into energy needed for daily life." It was once believed that eating too much sugar caused diabetes. This is not true. Although the actual cause of diabetes remains unknown, medical experts believe that heredity and lifestyle factors contribute to its onset.

There are two major types of diabetes (*Diabetes mellitus*):

- *Type 1 diabetes:* This form of diabetes is common in children and young adults, so much so that it used to be called "juvenile diabetes." In type 1 diabetes, the body does not produce insulin.
- *Type 2 diabetes:* This is the most common form of diabetes. Those with type 2 diabetes either do not produce enough insulin or the cells in the body fail to recognize insulin. The body's cells suffer because they are starved for the energy that they need. Type 2 diabetes tends to be a more common occurrence in African Americans, Latinos, Native Americans,

Asians, and the elderly. Adults who do not get enough exercise and are overweight, regardless of ethnic background, are particularly at risk of developing this type of diabetes.

Diabetes is a serious disease and there is no known cure. Some of the complications associated with diabetes are hyperglycemia, hypoglycemia, heart and kidney disease, and blindness. However, many with this disease live long and productive lives! Proper diagnosis and treatment are important keys to successfully living with diabetes.

Diabetes is a disease that affects 18.2 million people in the United States—5 million of whom are unaware that they even have it! For more information, including a quick "risk test," visit www.diabetes.org/home.jsp.

Why do onions make you cry?

Onions contain sulfur compounds which, when released into the air through cutting or otherwise damaging the bulb, are very irritating to the eyes. Tears are your body's response and they wash away the substance before it can affect or hurt the eye. To help reduce irritation when preparing onions, many cooks cut onions under a stream of cold water; others put onions in the refrigerator or freezer for a few minutes prior to cutting them. Some cooks recommend cutting the area closest to the roots last as there seems to be a greater concentration of the sulfur enzymes in that region of the onion bulb. Scientists believe that the same compounds that cause your eyes to tear are the same that give onions their distinctive and pungent taste.

Believed to have first been cultivated in Asia and the Middle East, onions have been eaten for thousands of years. Onions are nutritious. Among other things, they contain antioxidants, are low in calories, are fat free, and contain vitamins B and C. The average American today consumes more than 18 pounds of onions every year. Served fried, broiled, baked, or raw, onions are one of our most versatile foods by themselves or as an ingredient in many main or side dishes. Onions are also available in powdered or flaked form as well as frozen in your grocer's freezer. Perhaps you can think of additional ways to eat onions!

Onions are related to the lily. They are most often seen in red, yellow, and white varieties. The name, *onion*, is derived from the Latin *onus*, meaning unity or one. This makes sense when you consider the *oneness* of the many layers of an onion.

What is a pygmy?

The term *pygmy* (*pig*-me) may refer to several things. In general, it means a person, plant, animal, or thing that is small, particularly anything of unusually small size. Examples include the pygmy goat, pygmy hippopotamus, pygmy goose, and pygmy cypress. The term may also be used as an insult to signify or describe a person considered unimportant or insignificant.

Perhaps the most widely known use is as a reference to the pygmy peoples of Africa. Ranging in height from less than 4 feet to about 5 feet, African pygmies live in the great forests of the continent's equatorial regions and are known for their hunting and foraging skills. There are multiple populations of pygmies that differ in varying degrees in ethnicity, language, and social, culinary, and cultural ways.

What is blood pressure?

Blood pressure is the force that your blood exerts against the walls of your arteries when your heart beats (systolic pressure) and when your heart rests between beats (diastolic pressure). Maintaining a blood pressure measurement that is within normal limits is important to one's overall health. Fortunately, measuring blood pressure is quick, easy, and painless. Using a sphygmomanometer (*sfig*-mow-mah-*no*-meh-ter) and a stethoscope, your doctor or nurse can hear your blood traveling through your artery and measure your blood pressure. Digital cuffs are also available. Blood pressure is measured in millimeters of mercury (mmHg) and referred to as two numbers—systolic pressure, then diastolic pressure. If you ask what your blood pressure reading is, the answer will be described to you as something like, "120 over 75."

High blood pressure, called hypertension, is a serious health concern. According to the American Heart Association, high blood pressure is considered to be a blood pressure measured greater than or equal to 140 mmHg over greater than or equal to 90 mmHg. People with high blood pressure are at greater risk for heart disease, heart attack, and stroke. Children can have high blood pressure, but it is far more common in adults 35 years of age or older, especially those who drink alcohol heavily, are overweight, are women who take certain medications, or have diabetes, gout, or kidney disease. African Americans seem to be at greater risk, too.

Over 50 million Americans have high blood pressure. Most people experience no symptoms when they have high blood pressure. This is why hypertension is often referred to as the "silent killer." Fortunately, there are things we can do to maintain a normal blood pressure. Eating a healthy diet, exercising, limiting sodium intake, limiting alcohol consumption, and not smoking all contribute to lowering one's blood pressure. Your doctor may also prescribe certain medications to help control high blood pressure in conjunction with healthy lifestyle choices.

Who was General Tom Thumb?

Charles Sherwood Stratton was born in Bridgeport, Connecticut, in 1838. He is believed to have been born with a condition now referred to as *proportionate dwarfism*. Standing only 25 inches tall and weighing approximately 15 pounds at the age of four, he was "discovered" by the famed P. T. Barnum, who offered his parents a contract to let the child be exhibited as a human curiosity. They agreed to the deal. Charles began a new life with a new name, "General Tom Thumb," the name undoubtedly inspired by the nursery rhyme character. Barnum oversaw Thumb's education, which included the three Rs and learning how to sing, dance, act, mime, and, of course, the finer points of showmanship. In fact, Thumb was considered to be most entertaining when impersonating historical figures. Napoleon Bonaparte was a favorite subject for these purposes.

While considered repugnant today, the practice of exhibiting individuals with physical differences in circuses, fairs, and other types of traveling shows for entertainment and amusement was common in the 19th century. This sort of display widely appealed to the masses, royalty, heads of state, and the wealthy alike. Barnum and Thumb created quite a sensation when they toured America, France, England, Greece, and many other countries. Thumb met, among others, Britain's Queen Victoria, France's King Louis Philippe, and President Abraham Lincoln through his travels. Barnum and Thumb were friends as well as colleagues and became quite famous and wealthy.

In 1863 Thumb married a fellow Barnum employee, Lavinia Warren (also born with proportionate dwarfism) in a well-publicized and lavish ceremony in New York City. After their marriage, they toured with Barnum as top attractions until their retirement. Although the couple never had children, Barnum regularly "provided" them with an infant for publicity purposes. General Tom Thumb died of a stroke in 1883. At his death, he was said to have stood 40 inches high, weighing in at 70 pounds.

What is smallpox?

Smallpox is a serious, disfiguring, contagious disease caused by the variola virus. Approximately 30% of those who contract smallpox perish. Some forms of the disease are almost always fatal. Typically transmitted person to person through the air by sneezing, coughing, or talking, smallpox can also be contracted through direct contact with infected body fluids and items such as contaminated clothing and bed linens. According to the Centers for Disease Control and Prevention (CDC) in Atlanta, initial symptoms of smallpox include fever, head and body aches, and sometimes vomiting. Red spots that turn into erupting sores appear on the tongue and in the mouth. A rash appears on the face and spreads to all parts of the body. This rash becomes raised bumps that fill with clear fluid, then pus, which eventually scab over. Most bumps will develop a depressed area, a telltale characteristic of smallpox. These pustules are typically very painful and are often described as feeling like BB pellets under the skin. After the scabs fall off, the skin beneath is usually deeply pitted and scarred. Survivors are immune to future contraction of smallpox.

There is no cure for smallpox; only vaccination as a preventative has been found to stop this terrible disease. Fortunately, due to an aggressive vaccination campaign, smallpox is currently considered to be eradicated worldwide. The last case was diagnosed in the United States in 1949; the last naturally occurring case elsewhere was in Somalia (Africa) in 1977. Because of this, routine vaccinations for smallpox were deemed no longer necessary and were therefore discontinued.

After the terrorist attacks of September 11, 2001, the issue of bioterrorism (intentionally using a disease-causing agent to infect others) arose. Officially, stocks of the live smallpox virus are now maintained for scientific purposes at the CDC and at a secure lab in Siberia. However, there is a great deal of concern that the virus may exist in other places where security and intent for use are questionable.

The United States currently has enough vaccine to vaccinate every American. Debate, however, surrounds the use of the vaccine as it contains live "vaccinia" virus, not dead virus as is used in many other vaccines. In the past, some people have had serious reactions to the smallpox vaccine and a few died. Because of this concern and no known immediate danger of attack, the U.S. government has not yet implemented a wide-scale vaccination program.

For more information on smallpox, visit www.mayoclinic.com or www.bt.cdc.gov.

What causes brain freeze?

Brain freeze and *ice cream headache* are commonly used terms for the intense and sudden headache you may get when you eat something cold, like ice cream or a snow cone, on a hot day. This is caused by the sudden change in temperature in your mouth. Nerves in the roof of your mouth essentially "overreact," causing a swelling (dilation) of the blood vessels that are trying to protect your brain by adding more warmth. Approximately 30% of the population experiences this type of pain which, fortunately, only lasts about 30 seconds. You can lessen this problem by eating cold items more slowly and by trying to keep cold food or drink away from the roof of your mouth—although that is easier said than done.

Why do we yawn?

Knowledge about yawning is incomplete. However, the prevailing medical explanation for yawning involves the body needing more oxygen in the blood and/or removing accumulations of carbon dioxide from the blood. This explanation, however, has been challenged by the research of Dr. Robert Provine, a psychologist from the University of Maryland, Baltimore County. His research involved having subjects breathe various mixtures of oxygen and carbon dioxide. Increasing the oxygen did not decrease the rate of yawning; increasing the level of carbon dioxide did not increase the rate of yawning. Yawns apparently may also be triggered by fatigue, drowsiness, or boredom.

Interesting facts about yawning:

- Cats, dogs, fish, reptiles, some birds, and many other animals yawn.
- Fetuses as young as 11 weeks old yawn.
- A yawn lasts approximately six seconds, with an increase in heart rate of as much as 30%.
- Athletes often yawn immediately prior to competition.
- The scientific term for "yawning and stretching" is *pandiculation*.
- Seeing someone else yawn will often trigger a yawn.
- Reading about yawning may cause yawning. (Didn't you notice?)

To learn more about yawning, visit http://faculty.washington.edu/chudler/yawning.html.

In scuba diving, what does it mean to have *the bends*?

The bends is a term for a very serious medical condition called *decompression sickness* (DCS). The air that we breathe on land is a mixture of gases, including nitrogen; the same is true of the air that is compressed in a diver's tank. During a dive, increased pressure from the surrounding water causes nitrogen from the air being breathed to dissolve into the diver's body tissues. The amount of nitrogen absorbed depends on how deep and how long the dive lasts. When the diver ascends (swims toward the surface), the pressure of the water decreases and the nitrogen starts to leave the body. This is a normal process that usually causes no problems if the diver follows recommended safety procedures.

However, if the diver stays underwater too long and/or the dive is too deep, excess nitrogen is absorbed and begins to form bubbles in blood vessels and tissues when the diver ascends—much like when a soft drink can is shaken and then opened quickly. These bubbles may, for example, press on nerves and tear small blood vessels. Symptoms of DCS may include joint pain, shock, dizziness, breathing difficulty, and paralysis. In the most severe cases, death occurs. Many incidences of DCS are treated by repressurizing the affected diver in a recompression chamber. Fortunately, with proper treatment, DCS is rarely fatal for the recreational diver.

Source: *PADI Open Water Diver Manual*, Professional Association of Diving Instructors.

What does it mean to be left brained or right brained?

The human brain is divided into two sides or hemispheres. Although both hemispheres work together, each side of the brain processes information differently and controls functions on the opposite side of the body. Brain research suggests that each side of the brain may also control different *styles* of thinking or learning. Much of the current research is based on the pioneering work of California Institute of Technology psychobiologist Dr. Roger Sperry, who discovered that the hemispheres of the brain "specialized" in different capacities. Sperry received the Nobel Prize for his research in 1981.

Learning characteristics often attributed to "right-brained" individuals (often left-handed) include problem solving, creativity, and learning visually and with hands-on activities. They may be gifted in the arts, dance, and music. "Left-brained" individuals (often right-handed) may be more logical, rational, and analytical in their thinking and learning. They may excel in math and science.

Most individuals show a preference for one or the other of these modes of thinking, although no one person is completely left brained or right brained. Research suggests that regardless of which side of the brain appears to be dominant in an individual, both sides can be further developed for a more "whole-brained" approach to learning.

To learn more about hemispheres of the brain, visit www. mtsu.edu/~devstud/advisor/hemis.html.

What is a uvula?

A uvula (*yoo*-vuh-luh) is that small, fingerlike, dangling tissue that hangs in your mouth at the back of your throat (soft palate). The word is taken from the Latin word for grape (*uva*). It serves important functions, such as in the articulation of words and in helping to prevent food from entering the breathing passage or nasal cavity.

Normally, the uvula does its job day in and day out without difficulty. However, it can contribute to snoring or other sleep-related problems or can become swollen, which may cause breathing, speaking, and eating problems.

How did the phrase *cold turkey* originate?

The phrase *cold turkey* originated in the early 20th century. Its original meaning was to undertake a task without prior preparation. It is thought that this was originally derived from the limited work needed to prepare a meal featuring leftover or cold turkey. Later, *cold turkey* became associated with a more disturbing meaning— the immediate and complete cessation from use of an addictive or unhealthy substance. *Cold turkey* as a phrase is linked to symptoms of withdrawal from certain drugs, such as heroin or morphine. During withdrawal, blood is drawn toward the body's internal organs. Goose bumps and paleness result, making the skin somewhat resemble a cold, plucked turkey.

The phrase today is most commonly used to describe giving up something abruptly. This can mean the more obvious drugs, alcohol, or nicotine, but it may also be used to signify almost any type of stoppage, such as a dieter going *cold turkey* by giving up sweets, carbs, or fried foods.

What does having 20/20 vision mean?

A vision score of 20/20 is what eye doctors and other health-care professionals consider to be *normal* or *standard* vision. It is an indicator, among others, of good eye health and represents a point of reference from which better or worse eyesight is determined. We are all familiar with the standard "big E" eye chart to test vision. It was developed by Dutch ophthalmologist Dr. Herman Snellen in 1862. Still used today, the Snellen Chart may feature variations, including letters, numbers, or pictures arranged in lines in decreasing size. The patient is asked to sit or stand in a place at a distance of 20 feet from the chart to read, indicate direction, or otherwise identify the figures present on certain lines of the chart. One eye is covered while the other eye is tested.

A fraction results from the distance (as numerator) and line read (as denominator). So, as a simple explanation, if you are standing 20 feet from the chart and you can read line 20 (font size = 43), you have what is called 20/20 vision. If you are at a distance of 20 feet and you can only read line 40 comfortably, you have 20/40 vision—poorer vision than the standard 20/20. If you are at a distance of 20 feet and you can read line 15 comfortably, you have 20/15 vision—sharper vision than the standard 20/20.

3

Language

What is an anagram?

Anagrams have been used as a form of amusement since ancient times. Throughout history, secrets have been coded within them and royals have been lampooned by them. The word *anagram* is taken from the Greek *ana*, "back or again" and *gram* (from *graphein*), "to write." An anagram is a type of word puzzle or word game where one can rearrange the letters in a word or phrase to say something else. The trick is that each letter in the original word or phrase can only be used once and all letters must be used. In their simplest form, anagrams are usually written in the form of an equation using the equal symbol (=). Examples of simple anagrams are:

- ❧ earth = heart
- ❧ Britney Spears = Presbyterians
- ❧ astronomers = moon starers
- ❧ Clint Eastwood = old west action

Ideally, anagrams produce a humorous connection. Today computers assist in developing and decoding anagrams, but purists insist on solving these puzzles without any assistance.

What is the difference between an acronym and an abbreviation?

An acronym (*ak*-ruh-nim) is a new, shorter word formed from the first letter of a series of words or by combining parts of words. The new word "stands" for the words from which it was formed. For example, NASA is the acronym for the National Aeronautics and Space Administration and NATO is the North Atlantic Treaty Organization. Coming from the Greek *acro* for "extreme end" or "tip" and *onyma* for "name," many acronyms are so commonly used we do not even think of them as acronyms, such as scuba (self-contained underwater breathing apparatus), AIDS (acquired immune deficiency syndrome), and radar (radio, detecting and ranging).

An abbreviation, from the Latin *brevis* for "short," is simply the shortening of a word or group of words, for example, NY, USA, MVP, etc., Dr., and mph. Notice that these examples do not form a word themselves. To complicate the matter, abbreviations that use the first initial of each word it represents, like ABC, NBC, CNN, IBM, and several of the abbreviations noted above are actually a special category of abbreviations called "initialisms." Although the terms *acronym*, *abbreviation*, and *initialism* are often used interchangeably, they are actually different, with their own distinct meanings.

What is an epigram?

Epigrams are short, witty poems or statements. They are believed to have been first used in ancient Greece as tombstone or monument inscriptions. Epigrams are characterized by a clever, often humorous, twist or turn of thought. Oscar Levant (1906–1972), well known in the media for his mordant humor, is quoted as saying, "an epigram is only a wisecrack that's played Carnegie Hall." Two examples of poetic epigrams are:

> Little strokes
> Fell great oaks.
>
> —Benjamin Franklin

> Here lies my wife: here let her lie!
> Now she's at rest—and so am I.
>
> —John Dryden

A nonpoetic epigram is exemplified by Oscar Wilde's, "I can resist everything except temptation."

What does *euphemism* mean?

According to the *Merriam-Webster Dictionary*, the word *euphemism* (*you*-fem-izm) is "the substitution of an agreeable or inoffensive expression for one that may offend or suggest something unpleasant." Roughly translated from the Greek as "speech that sounds good," euphemisms tend to soften or be more indirect when referring to a specific thing or situation. The term is believed to have been first used around 1681. Some examples of euphemisms and their corresponding "translations" are:

* May I be excused? *May I go to the bathroom?*
* Pardon my French. *Pardon my use of bad words.*
* The departed is my cousin. *The dead person is my cousin.*
* I found myself in reduced circumstances. *I found myself poor.*

❧ I got up on the wrong side of the bed. *I am being crabby and am in a bad mood.*

What is an oxymoron?

According to the *Merriam-Webster Collegiate Dictionary* (10th edition), an oxymoron is "a combination of contradictory or incongruous words." The correct plural form of *oxymoron* is *oxymora*, although "oxymorons" is frequently used. The word *oxymoron* itself is an oxymoron as its roots come from the ancient Greek *oxys* (sharp/keen) and *moros* (dull/foolish). The words in an oxymoron are usually opposites and/or words not normally used together. We use oxymora often in our everyday speech; they make perfect sense to us when we use them. Examples of oxymora are jumbo shrimp, quite a few, grand theft, half dead, double solitaire, sanitary landfill, and virtual reality. Sentences, too, can be oxymoronic. Mark Twain once said, "it usually takes more than three weeks to prepare a good impromptu speech."

What is a palindrome?

A palindrome is a word, number, sentence, or verse that reads exactly the same way forward that it does backward. The first palindromes are believed to have been written by Sotades of Maronea, a Greek poet living in Egypt in the third century BC during the reign of Ptolemy II. As punishment for deeply offending the king with an insulting palindrome verse, Sotades was encased in a lead chest and cast into the sea. Although the story is not substantiated, Ptolemy is reported to have said, "Try reversing that one, pal!" Simple examples of palindromes are:

- racecar
- civic
- mom
- radar
- deed
- pup
- eye
- dad
- kayak
- 1991
- 2002
- level

Punctuation and spacing are often ignored when reading a palindrome in reverse. This is demonstrated in the following famous palindrome phrases:

- A man, a plan, a canal: Panama (Leigh Mercer, to honor Theodore Roosevelt)
- Madam, I'm Adam (Mark Twain)

What is a spoonerism?

A spoonerism results when one transposes or switches the first (usually) sounds, syllables, or letters of words in a phrase. These slips of the tongue often create new words or sentences. Some examples are:

- I will follow the plaster man (master plan).
- She looked in the cabinet for the snail tracks (trail snacks).
- The usher told us he would sew us to our sheets (show us to our seats).

The term *spoonerism* is taken directly from the misstatements of William Archibald Spooner (1844–1930), an Anglican priest and scholar. Spooner was a small, albino man with poor eyesight. He is said to have been a kind, gentle, and hospitable man. Quite intelligent, he became known for his frequent, humorous transpositions which occurred at any point in time, especially when he was agitated. Among his many widely known spoonerisms was, when prompting a shy bridegroom, "Son, it is now kisstomary to cuss the bride." He is also credited with saying (to the dean's secretary), "Is the bean dizzy?" Another slip occurred when he asked his congregation to sing "Kinkering Congs Their Titles Take," meaning to say instead, "Conquering Kings."

What is the meaning and origin of *gobbledygook*?

Gobbledygook (sometimes spelled gobbledegook) was coined in 1944 by Maury Maverick (1895–1965), a Democratic member of the U.S. House of Representatives and chairperson of the Smaller War Plants Corporation during World War II. He is credited with originating the nonsense word *gobbledygook* to describe bureaucratic jargon, doubletalk, and/or something described in an overly complicated or artificially pompous fashion. Maverick ascribed making up this word by observing turkeys on his farm, "always gobbledy gobbling and strutting with ludicrous pomposity."

Interestingly, gobbledygook is the language "spoken" by the goblins in Harry Potter novels.

What is the origin of the phrase *apple of my eye*?

To be the apple of one's eye is to be a precious person or thing in the eye of the beholder. The phrase is often used to refer to a child, grandchild, or significant other. The phrase has its origins in a misunderstanding of human anatomy. Early anatomists believed that the eye's pupil was a hard, round organ central to the overall physical well-being of the person. It is believed that because the apple was a commonly known fruit and had a roughly spherical shape, what is called the pupil of the eye today became known as the *apple of the eye* then. In addition, one's sight was regarded as the most valued sense; therefore, the analogy of being coveted, valued, or held precious rang true then, as it does today.

The phrase has been used for thousands of years, as documented in Deuteronomy 32:10 (He guarded him as the apple of his eye) and in Psalm 17:8 (Keep me as the apple of your eye; hide me in the shadow of your wings). The phrase is also seen in secular works as early as the ninth century and later in Shakespeare's *A Midsummer Night's Dream*.

What does it mean *to have an albatross around one's neck*?

To have an albatross around the neck means that one is burdened by an annoying or troubling problem or that one is experiencing some sort of obstacle to success (usually self-inflicted). The phrase originates in Samuel Taylor Coleridge's poem "The Rime of the Ancient Mariner." In the poem, the mariner kills a harmless albatross, a bird considered to be a good omen for the ship's safety. As punishment, the ancient mariner is forced to wear the dead bird around his neck.

An albatross is a large sea bird typically found in the Southern Hemisphere. They are large, web-footed birds characterized by a hooked beak and long, narrow wings.

Modern uses of the phrase may include:

- Paying for our house on the beach is an albatross around my neck.
- He needs to dump his girlfriend because she really is an albatross around his neck.

What does the phrase *rank and file* mean?

Rank and file is an expression of military origin, where in parade-ground terminology a *rank* refers to soldiers standing side by side in a row, and *file* refers to soldiers standing behind one another in a column. Its first known figurative use, that is—beyond that of the military—is believed to be around 1860.

Today, rank and file is probably most often used to describe the body of workers in a labor union, but it can also be used in reference to any group of everyday people. Other common uses for this phrase are to denote either enlisted troops in an army (exclusive of commissioned and noncommissioned officers) or the people who constitute the majority of any organization, group, or business (exclusive of managers, owners, or administration).

What is meant by *salad days*?

The idiom *salad days* refers to one's youth or a time in life characterized by happiness, indiscretion, and/or inexperience. This phrase was originated by William Shakespeare in *Antony and Cleopatra*. Speaking of herself, Cleopatra says, "my salad days, when I was green in judgment." She is speaking of her youthful infatuation with Julius Caesar—*green* referring to her own inexperience and, of course, the color of salad.

Examples of usage include:

» How I miss the salad days of my college years!

» My salad days were spent in Nebraska on my parents' farm.

» Perhaps I can recapture memories of my salad days by walking barefoot in the sand.

Where did the phrase *chip off the old block* originate?

The phrase *chip of the same block* is known to have been used in a sermon delivered by Dr. Robert Sanderson, Bishop of Lincoln (England) in 1637, referring to his relationship with Adam. Other versions meaning the same thing are also recorded back to ancient times (Theocritus' use of "a chip of the old flint" in 270 BC, for example). Time modified its usage to the now familiar "chip off the old block"—an expression that universally means a person that looks or acts like one or both parents or close associates. The modern interpretation undoubtedly has an association with carpentry, a chip coming from a block of wood. One example of usage is:

❧ It is no wonder that he won the race. He is a chip off the old block when you consider that his father was a marathon runner.

What is an Achilles' heel?

Everyone has weaknesses—physical, emotional, intellectual, and/or others. The phrase *Achilles' heel* is used in contemporary language to describe a point of weakness or vulnerability in someone or something. For example:

❧ The airplane that we built is beautiful, but we must examine its engine for any Achilles' heels.
❧ She is just too good to be true; surely she has an Achilles' heel.

Achilles' heel originates from Greek mythology. Interestingly, in Homer's *Iliad*, Achilles' weakness was his pride. It was the Roman poet Statius who wrote of the tale of Achilles and the River Styx. When Achilles was born, his mother, Thetis, desired to make him immortal. It was reputed that the waters of Styx, a poisonous underworld river, held such supernatural powers, so she took him to the riverbank and, holding him by his heel, dipped him in the river. Later, he was mortally wounded in the Trojan War by an injury to his heel—the heel that remained untouched by the river water because of his mother's grasp on it.

Why are the British called *limeys* and *blokes*?

Limey originated as 19th-century American and Canadian slang for British sailors. It originated with the practice that the Royal Navy and the Merchant Navy had of providing their sailors with lime juice to help prevent scurvy, a disease caused by a lack of vitamin C and characterized by swollen and bleeding gums and bleeding under the skin. British sailors were originally nicknamed *lime-juicers*, which in time was shortened to *limeys*. This term, generalized and softened somewhat, is still slang with a negative connotation that refers to any English person.

Bloke (*bloak*) refers to a man, usually in a friendly fashion (for example, "James is a great bloke to have with you on a long trip"). Typically, *bloke* implies simply being an ordinary, everyday sort of guy, but sometimes it may also be used in a negative way if one considers oneself to be superior in some way. ("He is terribly bloke-ish, always talking about sports and hunting dogs.") *Bloke* is thought to have originated from the Dutch *blok* (fool) and/or Shelta *loke* (man).

How did jaywalking get its name?

Jaywalking is typically defined as a pedestrian crossing a street at a place that is not a corner or at a place that is not designated for crossing by a crosswalk, signal light, or sign. Many municipalities consider jaywalking to be a misdemeanor offense that may result in a fine levied against the jaywalker. For centuries, the word *jay* has been used colloquially for a person who is foolish, dull, or unsophisticated. During the late 19th and early 20th centuries, places or things were often described as *jay* as well—jay town (country town) or jay train (riding in the cars reserved for poorer patrons), for example. The term *jaywalker* came into common usage in 1917 in Boston, when it appeared in *Harper's Magazine* describing pedestrians who foolishly disobeyed newly created traffic rules.

What is a straw man?

The term *straw man* (sometimes *strawman*, *straw-man*, or *man of straw*) has many applications and can be a person, argument, transaction, or document that is intended in some way to be weak or to mask a true situation. A straw man can be a person in whose name a business transaction takes place in order to hide the true man or woman behind the deal. Similarly, it can be used to signify someone who appears to be in charge of an organization or situation, but in reality, someone else is. It can also be an argument or issue used to hide the true problem or situation and/or to divert attention from real or important issues. *Straw man* is also a tactical strategy often used in politics and law, for example, to cite a portion or an area of weakness in an opponent's point of view, then refute or discredit it as if the opponent's actual or total argument was refuted. Yet another usage is in decision-making situations when a draft proposal or prototype is made to serve as a starting point—one where weaknesses are expected to be exposed in order to correct and strengthen the document or object.

It is almost certain that our use of *straw man* originated from the practice of using what we now call a scarecrow, a figure dressed to resemble a person to frighten unwanted intruders from one's garden. In other words, a scarecrow looks like something it is not. In literature, this usage was reinforced in Heinrich Mann's *Man of Straw* (1918). In it, the main character (Diederich Hessling) portrays himself a man of strong ideals and commitment, yet his actions and practices belie this. He espouses bravery, yet his cowardice is quite apparent and his promotion of military valor is countered by the fact that he seeks an early dismissal from his military service.

What is hyperbole?

Hyperbole (hi-*pur*-buh-lee) is an exaggeration, overstatement, or embellishment of an event or occurrence. It is a figurative language used to stress importance, to emphasize something, or to impress someone with the depth of one's feelings or opinions. The key to differentiating a hyperbole from other figures of speech is the element of exaggeration. For example:

- ☙ I almost died laughing at that joke.
- ☙ When she got home from school, the student told her mother how she told the principal how to run that school!
- ☙ The angler claimed that the fish he lost was as big as a truck.

The word *hyperbole* itself can be used as follows:
- ☙ Caught in the act, Jeffrey was prone to hyperbole when extolling his innocence to his father.
- ☙ The attorney used hyperbole to present her client to the jury in the best possible light.

What does it mean to blackball someone?

This term originated from a practice used in the past by many private clubs and organizations. Membership or other functions were voted on anonymously by participants casting a vote for or against someone or something by placing a white (or some other color) ball or marble into the container to signify "yes" or a black ball or marble to signify "no." To be blackballed meant that the prospective member received one or more black balls or marbles.

Although this practice is no longer common, the phrase lives on meaning the same as it did when votes were cast in this fashion— that a person is denied membership or access to a position or that a decision or issue is denied. Contemporary usage of *blackball* may include:

- ☙ I really wanted to participate in the marathon, but the organizers must have blackballed me.

> ‣ Although most of the employees wanted to institute a "casual Friday" dress code at work, the boss blackballed the idea.

What is schadenfreude?

Schadenfreude (*shod*-un-froy-duh) is a feeling of pleasure or joy resulting from the misfortune of another. It is a word of direct German origin from *schaden* (damage) and *freude* (joy). It is used as a noun as follows:

> ‣ Annie couldn't help feeling schadenfreude when her classmate got in trouble with the teacher.
> ‣ They knew it was schadenfreude, but the employees were inwardly happy to hear that their lazy boss was about to be fired by the governing board.

What does being *long in the tooth* mean?

The phrase *long in the tooth* is used to signify that one is aging, elderly, or too old (in the opinion of others) for a given activity. It can also mean that one is wise. The expression dates back to at least 16th-century England and refers to the sale of horses. As horses age, their gums recede, which makes it appear as if the horse's teeth are growing longer! To avoid being cheated, those purchasing a horse would typically check the horse's teeth to get a reasonably accurate idea of the age or health, and therefore value, of the animal. Contemporary examples of usage include:

- The participants at the concert appeared to be a bit long in the tooth.
- To better understand life's mysteries, I recommend that you consult Mr. Edwards, who is getting long in the tooth.
- At 35, Jackson was getting too long in the tooth to be skateboarding.

Closely related to *long in the tooth* is the expression, *don't look a gift horse in the mouth*. Derived from the same practice of checking the teeth of a horse, it implies that one should not overly examine a gift or disappointment may follow.

What does *to smell a rat* mean?

Idioms add such wonderful texture to our language. When someone says, "I smell a rat," they obviously do not mean that they physically smell the aroma of this particular rodent! This phrase dates back to at least the 1500s and typically means that one perceives something is wrong with a situation. Often there is no proof of wrongdoing, but past experience or just that intuitive feeling that something is not quite right nags at us. Examples are:

- When her husband suddenly showed interest in purchasing her a diamond bracelet, the wife smelled a rat.
- I smelled a rat when I saw two antagonistic coworkers suddenly become friendly with each other.

Although the domesticated rat can certainly make a good pet, most societies consider rats in general to be notorious carriers of disease and pestilence, a filthy pest at the very least. Great lengths have been and are taken to rid homes, businesses, ships, and other venues of their presence. Many people maintain cats or ratters (rat-hunting dogs) on their property to rid one's castle (or hut) of rats and other rodents. Cats and ratters can often detect the movements or presence of rodents well before humans can and suddenly spring into action to seek and destroy them. When this occurs, the animal can appear to be reacting to nothing at all, thus giving rise to the idiom—*smelling a rat.*

What is a bête noire?

Bête noire (*bet*-nwahr) is a French phrase that translates as "black beast." It is used to identify someone or something that is unpleasant, dreaded, or disliked. Synonyms include bugbear, anathema, or abhorrence. Examples of usage are:

- Justin was an overall good student, but mathematics proved to be his bête noire.
- My sister-in-law is my bête noire, always criticizing my housekeeping and cooking skills.

What is the origin of the word *posh*?

Most of us associate the word *posh* with things or conditions that are luxurious, elegant, or fashionable. (For example, Donald Trump's condominiums in Miami are quite posh!) The origin of the word, however, is clouded. It is widely believed that the word originated as a term associated with the Peninsular and Oriental Steam Navigation Company (P&O Company), which served as a passenger carrier from England to India from 1842 to 1970. (The company is still quite active today, but in international cargo transport.) It is said that the most desirable passenger cabins were on the port (left) side of the ship going to India (Port, Out) and on the starboard (right) side from India back to England (Starboard, Home), and POSH is an acronym for these designations. These cabins received morning sun and afternoon shade, making them cooler overall than most other cabins. Eyewitnesses claimed that "POSH" was written on their boarding tickets in lavender ink. However, no such tickets have been found to corroborate this. In addition, records from the P&O Company do not indicate the use of this cabin designation, nor is it a recollection of former employees of the shipping company. It is speculated that "POSH" may have become unofficial, yet descriptive, terminology to indicate the aforementioned cabins by British and American passengers on this particular route.

Evidence of other early use of the word *posh* has appeared in various venues, such as in a cartoon in 1918, in turn-of-the-century dictionaries, and in Romany, the language of the Roma, as a monetary term. All of these possible origins point to an association with wealth or high fashion, but the definitive origin of the word *posh* remains a mystery.

Where did the phrase *slow as molasses* come from?

The phrase *slow as molasses* is a simile. A simile is a figure of speech that expresses a similarity or resemblance between things. Examples include being "big as a bus," "bright as day," or "black as night." It is quite common to make comparisons in our language and writing using similes. People in Victorian times often played a parlor game called Similes.

The original, and still used, phrase is "as slow as molasses in January." For starters, molasses in its purest form is made from sugarcane juice. It is a dark, thick, sweet syrup used in baking or as a condiment. Different grades of molasses can be produced depending on the maturity of the sugarcane, the amount of sugar extracted from it, and/or the method of processing.

Second, molasses is quite viscous. This means that it resists flowing smoothly and evenly due to the force that holds the molecules of molasses together. Consider the difference in "pourability" between water and catsup! Catsup is considerably more viscous. Viscosity *increases* as the temperature *decreases*. Therefore, cold molasses pours more slowly than warm molasses. Putting all of this together, we see that molasses (already a slow-moving liquid) is made even more slow by the coldness of January! Some examples are:

- The driver became impatient with the car in front of him, muttering that the other driver was as slow as molasses!
- Mr. Edwards hated to shop with his wife, knowing that she was as slow as molasses when there was a sale in progress.

What does *tête-à-tête* mean?

This French phrase (tate-a-*tate*) is often used in the United States without the accent marks and means literally "head to head." It is used to describe a private or intimate conversation between two people. It almost always implies a certain familiarity between the conversants or a conversation where an understanding or an exchange of views is desired. By extension, it may also refer to a short sofa which is built to seat two people. Examples of usage are:

- ✽ The president negotiated a new peace treaty as a result of a tête-à-tête he had with the prime minister of the rival country.
- ✽ Rhonda was anxious to have a tête-à-tête with Eric to resolve their differences.
- ✽ The engaged couple enjoyed having a tête-à-tête while sitting in the park watching the sun set.

What is a juggernaut?

Juggernaut (*jug*-er-nawt) is derived from the Sanskrit word *Jagannatha*, meaning "lord of the world." It is a title for the Hindu deity Krishna. The likeness of Krishna is drawn through the streets on a large cart during an annual procession of chariots. This festival began in India, but is now celebrated in many cities throughout the world. The frenzy of the crowd to see Krishna and other deities is so great that some spectators by choice or by chance have fallen and been crushed under the wheels of the cart.

In the United States, *juggernaut* is a word used to describe a force or thing that is unstoppable, crushing everything in its path. It can also be used to describe a belief or institution that elicits fervent or blind devotion to it, often to the detriment or extreme sacrifice of the follower. Large, unwieldy, or powerful vehicles can also be referred to as juggernauts. Examples of usage are:

- ✽ Serena and Venus Williams, tennis juggernauts, are formidable opponents on a clay court.
- ✽ The juggernaut of public opinion made it impossible for the

corporation to continue making the product with inferior materials.

❧ The juggernaut SS *Titanic* was considered an engineering masterpiece prior to its ill-fated maiden voyage.

What is a baker's dozen?

A *baker's dozen* is a phrase used for a group of 13. Although of "baking" origin, we often use this phrase today to refer to 13 of anything. The origin of this phrase is twofold.

Back in the Middle Ages, some unscrupulous bakers would cheat their customers by baking bread that had a great deal of air pockets. Such bread, naturally, had less substance to it and was lighter in weight. Because of this problem, the English passed laws in 1266 to regulate the weight of bread and provided stiff penalties for bakers who "short weighted" their customers. In an attempt to avoid sanctions, bakers and other tradespersons would often add an extra item "just to be sure." In addition to this, bakers would often sell loaves of bread to bread vendors. Because the weight and price were so strictly regulated, in times of plenty, bakers would give these vendors an extra item or piece per dozen to allow more profit for the vendor.

What is the difference in meaning between *biannual* and *biennial*?

The use of these two words can be tricky and they are often mis-used. To differentiate between the two words, think about the root word *ann*, meaning "year." The prefix *bi-* means two. Bicycle (two wheeled) or bicep (muscle having two points of origin) are examples of this usage. Therefore, biannual means something that is done two times in one year. Consider the following sentence: We take our biannual vacations to Florida in January and in July. The word *semiannual* is often used instead of biannual to help avoid confusion.

A biennial event occurs every two years. The root word *enn* means "years" (plural). So *biennial* means "two years." For example: The civic club elects officers biennially. The officers elected in 2008 will run for reelection in 2010. Another common use for biennial regards plants. A biennial plant (such as foxglove and carrots) lives for two years.

A key to remembering the meaning of these two similar words is remembering the *ann* and *enn* root words.

What is a toady?

A toady, according to the *American Heritage Dictionary of the English Language*, is a person who flatters or defers to others for self-serving reasons. Synonyms include bootlicker, apple polisher, fawner, and sycophant.

The word comes from the 17th-century belief that all toads were poisonous creatures. Charlatans who traveled the country selling potions and elixirs would impress crowds by having an assistant swallow a toad (pretending, of course). The "toad eater" would feign distress by choking, gagging, and displaying other symptoms of being desperately ill. The charlatan "doctor" would then administer a product to neutralize or extract the toad poison. Naturally, the assistant experienced a remarkable recovery and, because of this, a great deal of magical potion was sold! Because being the toad-eating assistant to a charlatan was considered to be an undesirable occupation, the assistants came to negatively symbolize the type of individual that would do anything for another person for fame, favor, or profit. Over time, *toadeater* was shortened to *toady*.

What is the difference between flammable and inflammable?

Both words, *flammable* and *inflammable*, mean the same thing—something that easily burns. The confusion comes into the picture because we usually use the Latin prefix "in" to mean "not" or to negate something. Consider the words inconsistent (not consistent), intolerable (not tolerable), invisible (not visible), or indirect (not direct). In the case of inflammable, the *in-* (also of Latin origin) is used as an intensive prefix and means "to be able to." In other words, it is used as "inflame + *able*."

Because of the great need to be perfectly clear regarding flammable material, the terms "highly flammable" and "nonflammable" are typically used.

What is a quisling?

A quisling (*kwiz*-ling) is a traitor. The term is derived from Vidkun Quisling (1887–1945), a Norwegian army officer and politician, who collaborated with the Nazis during World War II. He helped Germany invade and conquer Norway. During the German occupation of Norway, Quisling was named minister president. When the Germans surrendered in 1945, the Norwegians arrested Quisling and convicted him of high treason. He was executed by a firing squad.

The word *quisling* is now used internationally as a term that means one who serves as a puppet or collaborator for an occupying enemy or one who betrays his or her country in some way. Synonyms for quisling include Benedict Arnold and Judas, other notable traitors.

What does it mean to have a *Hobson's choice*?

This is a phrase meaning that a choice offered, albeit a free choice, is not really a choice at all. The choice is usually either the thing being offered or nothing, or is between two similar and equally undesirable choices. This saying is thought to have originated in Cambridge, England, by stable keeper and courier Thomas Hobson (circa 1544–1631). It is said that Hobson would not allow individuals who wanted to hire one of his horses their choice of animal. He required that customers take the horse closest to the stable door or he wouldn't rent to the customer at all. The word about Hobson's rule spread and became known as Hobson's choice. Hobson was immortalized by the poet John Milton in two poems.

Today, the phrase rarely refers to horses but is still quite useful. Examples of its use are:

* Jeffrey's mother offered him the chance to apologize now or sit in time-out, and *then* apologize.
* Henry Ford offered his customers a choice of car colors, as long as the choice was black.

What does it mean when something is called a *red herring*?

For starters, a herring (*Clupea* sp.) is a fish found in great numbers in the North Atlantic Ocean. The fish is not red, but turns red or reddish when it undergoes a curing process called smoking. During this process, herring take on a strong and distinctive smell. As a food source, they are most often referred to as kippers or simply herring (not red herring).

The term *red herring* is an idiom typically used today to mean that someone is attempting to divert attention from the main issue, intentionally or accidentally. For example:

* The student moaned to her parents that her failing test grade was a result of not owning the latest computer (not the fact that she had not studied for the test).
* The politician urged his constituents to vote for the new gasoline tax increase, forewarning that without it the American way would be in jeopardy (not the fact that he had failed to explore alternative energy sources).

Synonyms for red herring include smoke screen, wild-goose chase, diversion, or deflection.

As with most phrases, *red herring* has several explanations as to its origin. The most direct and logical dates back to the use of red herring in a 1686 British publication, *The Gentleman's Recreation* by Nicholas Cox. For training dogs to hunt, Cox advocated dragging a dead cat or fox along a trail to mark (scent) it. If a dead cat or fox was unavailable, red herring was recommended.

It was also common in those days for criminals on the run to mark a trail with red herring to confuse and mislead any dogs in pursuit of them, meanwhile making their escape in another direction. Foxhunters, too, would occasionally mark certain hunting areas with red herring to temporarily deceive their hounds in order to prolong the foxhunt!

What is a soupçon?

The term *soupçon* (pronounced *soup*-sahn) means a small amount, a trace, a taste, a suggestion, or a slight addition to something. Usually this "small something" has a detectable effect on the object or thing that it influences. For example:

- ⚹ I detected a soupçon of sarcasm when she spoke to me.
- ⚹ I like my tea with a soupçon of cream.
- ⚹ The defendant did not show a soupçon of remorse.

The word itself is derived from the Old French word *sospeçon* (meaning suspicion), which was originally derived from the Latin *suspecti*. The "hook" on the letter *c* in soupçon is called a cedilla (sih-*dill*-uh).

Why are certain medications called *over-the-counter*?

To fully appreciate how this term came to be, remember that early apothecaries, drugstores, and pharmacies were not the multiaisle superstores that are so popular now. Most were small shops typically staffed by one person called an apothecary and later, a druggist or pharmacist. Medical preparations, ingredients, and equipment were typically kept on shelves or in a cabinet behind the shop's counter. Medicines at that time did not come premixed or prepackaged as most do today. Apothecaries had to grind and mix them, often from ingredients that they grew or prepared themselves. Medicines, whether ordered by a doctor or recommended by an apothecary, were purchased literally "over the apothecary's counter." The term, however, began to be associated with those medicines for which a doctor's prescription was *not* required. Today even though we can shop for many of these medicines ourselves in a store, we still refer to them as over-the-counter (OTC) medicines or drugs.

Today, the Federal Drug Administration (FDA) is responsible for deciding if a medicine is prescription (Rx) or nonprescription (OTC), and makes the decision to change a medication from Rx to OTC if warranted. Self-medication with OTC products is a 5 billion dollar per year business in the United States. Consumers should proceed with caution when selecting and using OTC medicines. Drug interactions, overdosing, and side effects can be problematic, even dangerous, if these products are misused or used in place of proper medical care.

What does *voir dire* mean?

The term *voir dire* (vwar-dear) is taken from the French language, and is roughly translated as "to speak truly, to tell the truth." It is widely used in the legal profession to describe a particular phase of jury selection in civil and criminal trials. Being judged by an impartial jury of our peers is a strong and clearly established principle of our legal system. During jury selection, the attorneys for each side (and sometimes the judge) have the opportunity to question jury candidates about their knowledge of the case, life experiences, opinions, and/or ability to render a fair and objective decision. Naturally, both the defense and the prosecution hope to select jurors who are sympathetic, or at the very least unbiased, toward their point of view. Certain prospective jurors can be dismissed by either side in accordance with specific guidelines. Those accepted by both sides become part of the jury.

What does *fait accompli* mean?

Fait accompli (*fayt* a-kom-*plee* or *fet*-a-kom-*plee*) is taken from the French language and means "an accomplished and/or irreversible fact, deed, or action." In other words—it is a done deal. Examples of usage are:

- ❧ He presented her with a fait accompli when he bought the new car without discussing the purchase.
- ❧ Don't tell me that you don't want me to marry him. We eloped to Las Vegas last week. It is a fait accompli!

What does *shedding crocodile tears* mean?

The use of the phrase *shedding crocodile tears* dates back to before the 13th century. It is thought to have originated because crocodiles tend to secrete eye fluid (tears) when they open their mouths, including, naturally, when they kill and swallow their prey. Because it may appear that the crocodile "cries" when feeding, it may be inferred that the crocodile feels sorry for its prey. This, of course, is not true. Therefore, the phrase "shedding crocodile tears" means

83

the display of false or hypocritical sorrow or the expression of insincere remorse or grief. It is also used for one who tries to gain sympathy or pity when no sympathy is called for or deserved. Examples of typical contemporary usage are:

- The teammates were simply shedding crocodile tears; they were all glad that Amy broke her leg and couldn't try out for the sport.
- Although the man wept at his wife's wake, he was accused of shedding crocodile tears when he was arrested for her murder.

What is the origin of the phrase *play it by ear*?

This phrase is what we call an "idiom." An idiom is a saying or phrase that uses words in a way that may seem unusual or illogical, but makes perfect sense in the culture that uses it. For example, when we say, "ouch, my dogs are barking," we are not talking about our pets disturbing the neighbors. We are saying that our feet hurt. Similarly, when we exclaim that we are going to "bury the hatchet" we are making peace with someone, unlike the literal translation, which would involve using a shovel!

Likewise, "play it by ear" is an idiom that means that we handle a situation in an impromptu fashion. We decide what to do as we go along without any specific guidelines or predetermined plan. It is thought that "play it by ear" originated from the field of music. Some musicians have the gift of being able to play a tune after simply hearing it. They do not need sheet music—hence, playing it by ear! Examples of ways to use this phrase are:

- I don't know when I can make the trip. I'll just have to play it by ear.

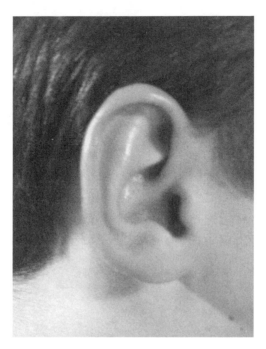

* Study for your test. Playing it by ear could have a negative impact on your grade!

What does *mea culpa* mean?

From the Latin language, *mea culpa* (*may*-uh *cull*-puh) is literally translated as "my fault." In other words, you admit that you are personally culpable or guilty of a certain action. When one uses this term, an apology, regret, and/or remorse is typically implied. Examples of usage are:

* My friend gossiped about me so I am waiting for her mea culpa.
* Did I say Athens is the capital of Georgia? Mea culpa! I meant Atlanta.

✮ Mea culpa. I can only say that I did not mean to offend anyone.

What does *pro bono* mean?

Translated from the Latin language, *pro bono* means "for the good." It is shortened from the phrase *pro bono publico* (for the public good) and is used primarily as legal terminology. Attorneys often give of their time and expertise by taking cases for which no compensation is expected nor requested. Encouraged by state and local bar associations, it is considered a desirable act of public service to accept certain cases for individuals who cannot afford an attorney and/or for those whose cases present a particular interest or challenge. Examples of usage are:

✮ The law firm took the case pro bono because the client was unable to pay for legal services.

✮ How could she possibly afford that famous attorney? They must have a pro bono arrangement.

In a deck of playing cards, why are jacks called jacks?

Playing cards have provided a popular pastime for centuries. Contemporary Anglo-American playing cards are a result of the French version featuring the four suits that we are familiar with (hearts, spades, clubs, and diamonds) and "court" or face cards (king, queen, and knave). The knave represents a valet or male servant and is the origin of the "jack" as we know it today.

At some point in the 1800s, the English version of knave began to be referred to as "Jack." This was considered to be a crass, if not

vulgar, usage, possibly from its association with the game All Fours, a card game popular particularly among the lower classes. For example, in Charles Dickens's *Great Expectations*, Estelle contemptuously criticizes Pip by saying, "he calls the knaves, Jacks, this boy! . . . And what coarse hands he has! And what thick boots!" In All Fours, the name of the point awarded for winning a trick containing the knave of trumps was *Jack*. The name *Jack* also applied to the knave of trumps itself. However, its usage got a shot in the arm in the mid-1800s, when cards started to be indexed (labeled on the corners to indicate the card's value) with K, Q, and Kn. To avoid confusion, "Jack" became the standard and most preferred method as *J* was more identifiable than *Kn*. Although the term "knave" was still used in card game books well into the 19th century, today we use the term *jack* almost universally.

What is the origin of the phrase *mind your p's and q's?*

A phrase that is now used to remind us to be on our best behavior and/or to be mindful of our manners has no clear origin. There are several popular and entertaining explanations.

The most likely origin comes from the pubs of 18th-century Great Britain. Ale was (and is) generally served by the pint or quart (not standard measures). Some patrons awaiting payday ran a bar tab which the bartender kept track of on a chalkboard by tallying p's and q's. When the bill got high enough, the bartender reminded the patron, "It is time to mind your p's and q's." Simply put, pay up! A variation of this version has the bartender shouting this phrase to those who, having had too many p's and q's, got rowdy in the pub. A third possibility involves the importance of remaining sober enough (and therefore exhibiting better behavior) so as not to be taken advantage of by dishonest bartenders who may pad the tick and/or charge for a quart when a pint had been ordered.

Another theory involves the difficulties faced by the now-defunct practice used by newspaper typesetters setting lower case p's and q's, which are easily confused due to their close physical resemblance. The same is true of children learning their alphabet.

A third option, albeit unlikely, is taken from the pronunciation similarity of p's to please and q's to thank you's.

What is the origin of the phrase *squared away?*

Many common phrases that we use today come from our nautical history. Examples include "knowing the ropes," "clearing the deck," and keeping things "on an even keel." The use of sailing ships was once the primary mode of sea transportation. Many types of square-rigged (sail) ships were used for travel, exploration, commerce, and military purposes. To sail the ship, sailors trimmed (adjusted) the sails in order to position the ship in the desired direction of travel (putting the ship before the wind). A ship that was "squared away" had "braced her yards (beams that supported the sails) before the wind." Over time, the phrase's meaning changed to include describing a ship that looked sharp or maneuvered capably, or sailor who was dressed to perfection or who performed a task or duty competently. The phrase is used today even more generally in all walks of life to mean being ready for action, prepared, tidy, or smartly dressed. Examples are:

- When his mom asked what his room looked like, he said that it was squared away.
- Having bought new clothing and a bottle of sunscreen, she was squared away for her vacation.

What does it mean to be blue-blooded?

According to *The American Heritage Dictionary of the English Language* (4th edition), the term *blue blood* is defined as: 1) noble rank or status by birth, or 2) people of the highest social level. *Blue-blooded* is often informally applied to those of royalty, aristocracy, nobility, or the upper crust of society. The term itself originated from the Spanish language for "blue blood" (*sangre azul*), and is believed to have been popularized by the older aristocratic families in Castile. Many of these families were lighter-skinned individuals of European origin. They declared themselves to be of pure ancestry having no genetic link with the darker-skinned Moors, Islamic warriors who invaded and occupied Spain from the eighth until the 13th centuries. Considering themselves to be superior to the Moors, they offered "proof" of this by pointing to their veins, which appeared bluish in color through their pale skin, thus distinguishing themselves from their Moorish conquerors. In time, the term *blue-*

blooded was adopted into use by the French (*sang bleu*), English, and others.

What is pin money?

For centuries, women have needed some type of fastener to hold their veils, wimples, and hats in place. Hatpins were used for this purpose. They were handmade, often ornate, and considered to be expensive luxury items. As manufacturing capabilities improved, the 19th-century British pin industry sought to protect against plummeting prices and imports from France by pressing Parliament to pass a law to restrict the sale of pins to the first two days in January. Women saved the allowances provided to them by their husbands or fathers all year to purchase pins, hence "pin money." Another explanation involves Queen Victoria, who collected taxes at the beginning of the year and was said to have timed this so that she could purchase *her* pins!

The use of hatpins has dramatically lessened during the past century. This has paralleled the widespread decline in the wearing of hats by women. The phrase "pin money" has endured, however, and is used today to describe money used to purchase small or incidental items and as a term meaning "pocket money" and/or money earned by a low-paying or part-time job.

What is a quidnunc?

A quidnunc (*kwid*-nunk) is a gossiper or inquisitive person. Coming from the Latin language, *quid nunc* means "what now." *Roget's II: The New Thesaurus* (3rd edition) refers to a quidnunc as being one who intrudes in another's affairs—a busybody, meddler, or, in slang terms, a buttinsky.

The term *quidnunc* was more widely used in yesteryear, notably in Sir Richard Steele's periodical *Tatler*, and in works by Nathaniel Hawthorne and Washington Irving. Well-known contemporary "professional" quidnuncs include gossip columnists Cindy Adams, Rona Barrett, and Liz Smith. A quidnunc, however, need not be a famous person. Perhaps you can think of quidnuncs among your own acquaintances!

What is the meaning of the phrase *good night, sleep tight, and don't let the bedbugs bite*?

Interpretations of this children's bedtime farewell vary. Some historians believe that "tight" refers to getting a *sound* night's sleep. Another widely held opinion involves the construction of the beds in colonial times. Beds had mattresses that were typically a cloth sack filled with animal hair, feathers, and/or straw. Having no box springs, ropes were stretched across the wooden bed frame to support the mattress. The ropes tended to sag under the weight of the bed's occupant and needed to be tightened periodically, hence "sleep tight."

Bedbugs are pests that have been well documented throughout recorded history. They feed off the blood of humans and certain other warm-blooded animals. As nocturnal insects, they come out of their hiding places and feast at night while their victims sleep. A bedbug bite appears as a small, hard, swollen, white welt that becomes red and itches intensely. Presumably, better hygiene, sanitation, and improvements in insect extermination have greatly decreased the incidence of bedbug problems.

What is a Pyrrhic victory?

A Pyrrhic (*peer*-ik) victory is a victory won at great cost—one that makes you wonder if you really won anything at all. It is an empty or hollow victory, at best. The phrase was reportedly coined in 1885 by a British newspaper, the *Daily Telegraph*, referencing King Pyrrhus of Epirus' victory against the Romans in 279 BC. During this battle, both sides combined lost approximately 15,000 men. When one of his men rejoiced at the victory, Pyrrhus reputedly remarked, "One more such victory and I am lost." Although he won that battle, he lost the war.

What does the phrase *quid pro quo* mean?

This phrase (kwid-pro-*kwo*) comes from the Latin language and translates as "something for something." Roughly, it means that one thing is given as compensation for another thing received. An example of this, although the actual phrase is not used, is:

* The palace allowed formal, staged pictures of Prince William to be taken in exchange (quid pro quo) for the media honoring his privacy on a day-to-day basis.

Another example that uses the phrase is taken from advice by Emily Post:

* The giving of personalized favors or small gifts to the guests at a wedding should not be considered as a quid pro quo for attending the occasion.

What does *cutting the Gordian knot* mean?

If you have *cut the Gordian knot*, you have used a bold, decisive solution to solve a difficult or complicated problem. The origin of this phrase comes from Greek legend. Gordius, king of Phrygia, tied the yoke of his wagon to a pole in front of his palace using an intricate knot. He did this primarily to remind himself of his humble origins. Following the death of his son, Midas, the knot was also instrumental in fulfilling the oracle's prophecy that he who was able to unfasten the knot would be the next ruler of Phrygia and of the vast lands of Asia. In 333 BC, Alexander the Great traveled through Phrygia and, like others before him, tried to untangle the knot. Unable to do so, he is said to have slashed the knot with his sword. Alexander the Great was crowned king and, in time, conquered Asia.

What did Marie Antoinette mean when she said, "Let them eat cake"?

Marie Antoinette was the Austrian-born wife of King Louis XVI of France. Although often described as extravagant, callous, and self-centered, she is probably not guilty of making this statement in response to being informed that many Parisians were starving. "Cake" in 18th-century France, incidentally, was a baker's term for a large, thick, flat piece of bread dough that had been baked until it was blackened and quite hard. This "cake" was then used as a buffer or base on which loaves of bread were baked, protecting them from the hot coals of the oven.

Historical scholars note that the "cake" statement was first printed by Jean-Jacques Rousseau in *The Confessions*, a book written several years before Marie Antoinette came to France to be married. Furthermore, Rousseau makes no reference to Marie Antoinette directly or indirectly in his book. Used by the enemies of the king and queen during the French Revolution, this statement was most likely taken out of context and attributed to the queen to further fan the flames of the people's dislike for her.

Convicted of treason on various charges, Marie Antoinette was guillotined on October 16, 1793.

What does the term *catch-22* mean?

Catch-22 is the title of a novel published in 1961 by American novelist and World War II veteran Joseph Heller. The story is a dark comedy focusing on death, insanity, and the absurdities of war. Set during the last months of World War II, the main character, Captain John Yossarian, seeks to stop flying bombing missions—but there is a catch. The catch is an unusual Army Air Corps regulation called "Catch-22." Essentially, Yossarian, a bombardier, would not be required to fly missions if he was crazy, but he had to *ask* to not fly missions to qualify. However, if he made the request to end his combat duty, this proved that he was sane and the missions had to continue! Either position taken—sane or insane—the air raid missions must go on.

The term "catch-22" is now used in American vernacular to express the condition of being caught in a no-win dilemma or situation. According to *Webster's New World College Dictionary*, catch-22 is defined as "a paradox in a law, regulation, or practice that makes one a victim of its provisions no matter what one does."

To learn more, visit www.cnn.com/1999/books/news/12/13/
heller/index.html.

What does it mean when something is called *the wreck of the Hesperus*?

This phrase is taken directly from Henry Wadsworth Longfellow's
poem, "The Wreck of the Hesperus." Longfellow (1807–1882) was
inspired to write this poem by the destruction of the schooner *Favorite* in 1839. In an area on the Massachusetts coastline known as
Norman's Woe, the site of many shipwrecks, the *Favorite* met her
fate; twenty bodies washed ashore, including that of a woman who
was bound to a piece of the schooner's wreckage. Longfellow, however, named the ship in his poem *Hesperus* after another vessel of
the same name that had been wrecked near Boston.

The poem tells the mournful tale of a skipper who took his
young daughter sailing upon the sea against the warnings of an old
seaman who foretold of an approaching hurricane (likely a nor'easter). As the storm began to rage, the skipper strapped his daughter
to the mast so that she would not be tossed into the sea. The skipper
perished in the storm. The next morning, fishermen found the body
of his daughter on shore, still lashed to the broken mast. This beautiful and haunting poem may be found at www.bartleby.com/42/
777.html.

Contemporary use of the poem's title typically refers to a thing
or situation being a disaster or a mess in some fashion. A parent,
for example, may use the phrase to describe a child's bedroom.

What does *the dog days of summer* mean?

We call the hot and humid days of late summer *the dog days*. This
period was identified as July 3 through August 11 by ancient

civilizations living around the Mediterranean Sea. Sirius (called the Dog Star) rose in tandem with the sun when summer was at its hottest. The ancients believed (erroneously) that because Sirius was such a bright star, it added to the heat normally generated by the sun, making these days even hotter. Therefore, this period of time began to be called the "dog days."

Today, the phrase *dog days* is often used to describe any period of hot and sultry weather typically extending beyond August 11. Interestingly, because people may tend to move more slowly and be less productive during these days, any time of stagnation may also be referred to as dog days. For example:

- Car salespersons often complain about the dog days of December when car sales are slow.

What is a quack?

A quack is an untrained person who practices medicine using methods, devices, or medicines known to be ineffective. The word has generalized in modern usage as pejorative slang for an incompetent medical doctor or one claiming to be a doctor, and in some cases, just an incompetent professional of any field. The word *quack* likely came from a modern use of the old Dutch *kwakzalver*—*kwak* (one who prattled or fussed about) plus *zalver* (used like our word salve or ointment). Therefore, a kwakzalver (quacksalver being the more contemporary Dutch word) was an individual who hawked potions or other remedies to cure all sorts of ills. Similar words are found in the German, Norwegian, and Old English languages. Synonyms for quack include charlatan, mountebank, and snake oil salesman.

What is meant by the *hoi polloi*?

Hoi polloi (*hoy*-pull-*loy*) is taken from the Greek meaning "the many" or "the common people." *Hoi* actually means "the." At one point it would have been considered incorrect to say "the" hoi polloi; however, it has been used this way for so long that saying "the hoi polloi" is now considered standard English usage. (In literature, hoi polloi may occasionally be found without "the" preceding it.) Hoi polloi is used interchangeably with mild to harsh pejoratives such as commoners, rabble, the masses, the proletariat, the huddled masses, plebeian, riffraff, and the like.

Interestingly, the term *hoi polloi* is often used incorrectly to signify the wealthy or upper crust, possibly being confused with phrases such as "hoity-toity." Examples of proper usage of hoi polloi are:

- ⚹ I only applied to the finest Ivy League schools to avoid dealing with the hoi polloi.
- ⚹ The dignitaries were disgusted with the attire and the deportment of the hoi polloi at the play.

What is a scapegoat?

The term *scapegoat* has a biblical origin. Leviticus 16 describes, as a customary part of the ceremonies of Yom Kippur (Day of Atonement), a ritual where the sins of the people were ceremonially heaped on the head of a goat. The goat was then driven off or allowed to escape, symbolically taking the sins of the people away as well. This scene is depicted in William Holman Hunt's (1827–1910) painting entitled *The Scapegoat*. *Scapegoat* means literally "escaping goat." The specific use of the word *scapegoat* is attributed to William Tyndale who in 1530 mistranslated the Hebrew word *Azazel*, an evil demon, for the Hebrew word for goat. The King James version still includes Tyndale's *scapegoat*; many contemporary translations use a corrected version.

Today, *scapegoat* is a term used to describe or name a person on whom responsibility for the mistakes of others is laid. For example:

- ⚹ We were all sorry to hear that Tony got fired; it was obvious that he was the scapegoat for the company's failure to perform well this quarter.

What is avoirdupois weight?

Avoirdupois (ahv-uhr-duh-*poyz* or *ahv*-uhr-duh-poyz) is the traditional system of weight in the United States. It was directly borrowed from the British system. The term is corrupted in pronunciation and spelling from the French *avoir de pois* (originally *aveir de peis*), which means *goods of weight*. This referred to goods sold by weight rather than by the piece. This system is based on the ancient system of the weight of a grain of wheat—with a pound equaling 7,000 grains. Avoirdupois weight includes the familiar measurements of ounce and pound. Units of measure in the avoirdupois system are multiples or fractions of the pound.

Interestingly, the term *avoirdupois* is also likely to be used in reference to one's personal weight. For example:

» My grandmother was a person of considerable avoirdupois.
» Upon looking at their wedding picture, the husband couldn't help commenting about the surplus avoirdupois that both had acquired over the years.

What does the phrase *the cat's meow* mean?

The cat's meow means that something or someone is outstanding in some way or simply too cool for words. It is synonymous with other phrases such as *the cat's pajamas* or *the bee's knees*. Examples of usage include:

- That outfit is the cat's meow.
- I love your car; it is the cat's meow.

The phrase was coined in the early part of the 20th century by Thomas A. Dorgan, an American cartoonist, journalist, and boxing expert. He is also credited with creating other slang words and expressions such as dumbbell (an unintelligent person), cheaters (reading glasses), hard-boiled (a tough or mean person), as busy as

a one-armed paperhanger (an overworked person), drugstore cowboy (a lazy person or a ladies' man), and many more. Although some consider these sayings somewhat outmoded, it is not uncommon to hear them used today.

Why do the British use the word *flat* for *apartment*?

Whereas it is true that *flat* is typically used in Great Britain for what Americans call an apartment, there is additional confusion in usage in both countries. For example, the English use the word *apartment* to describe a very posh flat or for rooms within a castle, palace, or other stately building occupied by royalty or a wealthy individual or family. Likewise, in America, the word *flat* may be used, typically in larger cities such as San Francisco or New York, to describe an apartment that consists of the entire floor of a residential building or a renovated multistoried home (much like in the UK). Some realtors consider ownership (rented vs. purchased) or form of entrance (private entrance vs. entrance within the building) as a factor in determining what this type of dwelling is called.

The word *flat* has been in widespread use in England as a type of housing since the 19th century. It may have been derived from the obsolete 15th-century Scottish word "flet," which means floor or the interior of one's home. Another alternative involves derivation from the Germanic root for the contemporary use of the adjective *flat*.

What is clear is that despite a common language, the British and Americans have distinct differences in vocabulary. For example:

British version: When I looked under the bonnet of my lorry, I realized that I needed to visit the ironmongery to purchase a torch and a spanner.

American translation: When I looked under the hood of my truck, I realized that I needed to visit the hardware store to purchase a flashlight and a wrench.

What is a sword of Damocles?

In classical mythology (as told by Cicero, a Roman politician and philosopher), Damocles was a courtier of the tyrant Dionysius II. Damocles persistently flattered Dionysius by complimenting his great wealth, power, and luxurious lifestyle. As a result, Dionysius asked Damocles if he would like a taste of what it was like to be a man of great riches and influence; Damocles was delighted to accept. Dionysius ordered the preparation of a sumptuous banquet in surroundings of unmatched splendor. Damocles enjoyed himself immensely until he noticed that a sword had been suspended above his head by a single horsehair. By doing this, Dionysius demonstrated to Damocles that great wealth and power was not what it may appear as it was fraught with worry, fear, and uncertainty. Damocles quickly decided that his "less fortunate" life was superior to that of Dionysius.

The predicament experienced by Damocles is echoed today in sayings such as "hanging by a thread" or "walking a mile in someone's shoes." The phrase *sword of Damocles* is defined as a threat, peril, or imminent danger. Examples of use are:

- The likelihood of violence hung over the neighborhood like a sword of Damocles.
- A sword of Damocles hung over her head every time she did not properly study for her final exams.

What does the phrase *tilting at windmills* mean?

The phrases *tilting at windmills* or *fighting windmills* both come from the novel *Don Quixote* (1605) by Miguel de Cervantes Saavedra. Scholars still debate whether the protagonist, Don Quixote, was mad, abundantly confused, or simply the victim of an overactive imagination. At one point, Quixote sees windmills in the distance and believes or mistakes them to be malevolent giants sent by evil enchanters. He proceeds to attack them—with predictable results.

Today, to say one is fighting windmills can mean one of several closely related things: 1) to attack an imaginary foe or threat; 2) to engage an opponent that cannot easily be defeated—if at all; 3) to fight a losing battle; or 4) to involve oneself in a noble, yet impossible, action. *Tilting* is a jousting term meaning to initiate combat or to attack an opponent, thus both phrases are essentially synonymous. Examples of usage are:

* The basketball team won the game despite most of the fans thinking that they were fighting windmills.
* He is simply tilting at windmills if he believes he will be offered a promotion within a year of employment.

What does *nipping something in the bud* mean?

Taken from horticultural roots (no pun intended), the phrase *nip it in the bud* likely originated by the common gardening practice of removing buds to encourage growth or production elsewhere on the plant, to direct growth in a desired direction, or to eliminate undesirable growth at an early stage of development. Gardeners know that if you take care of these needs when the growth is a bud, it is a far easier task than doing so later.

Today, although still a perfectly applicable garden phrase, *nipping something in the bud* is used to indicate dealing with a bad situation when it is small or to take action at the beginning of a problem before it gets out of hand. Examples of usage include:

- When she came home late from a date, her father grounded her to nip that behavior in the bud.
- When Marilyn saw finance charges on her bill, she cut up her credit cards to nip the temptation to spend in the bud.

What is the origin of the phrase *up to snuff*?

Up to snuff is a phrase that was derived from a certain form of tobacco use where powdered tobacco is inhaled through one's nostrils. Snuff use (called "taking snuff") was considered fashionable in early 19th-century England. It was typically used by wealthier persons as snuff was very expensive. The original phrase was *up to snuff and a pinch above it* and referred to one who was sharp, on the ball, or otherwise nobody's fool. It is unclear if the phrase referred to the quality of the tobacco, the status of the person typically using snuff, or the alert demeanor exhibited initially by the user after taking snuff.

Contemporary use of the phrase *up to snuff* generally means that one is capable, satisfactory in some way, or at least meets expectations. It is often used in a negative fashion as follows:

- The work ethic of the committee members was not up to snuff.
- Routine inspection of the bridges confirmed that some needed maintenance as they were not up to snuff.
- When given a choice of perfumes, Sally chose Chanel No. 5, declaring that the others were not up to snuff.

What is a confidence man?

A confidence man (also called a con man or scam artist) is someone, either male or female, who swindles others out of money or property, usually by gaining that person's trust or confidence. Many confidence games or scams are based on the innocent, albeit naive, victim believing that he or she will get rich quick. Another type of victim knowingly enters into an arrangement with a confidence man where they believe that they are part of the plan to extract money from others but are, in fact, swindled themselves! In these cases, the swindler becomes the swindled!

The term *confidence man* was coined based on the actions of William Thompson, a 19th-century criminal. Dressed in genteel fashion, Thompson would zero in on a wealthy New Yorker, gain his or her trust (confidence), then ask to "borrow" jewelry, money, or timepieces—never to be seen by the victim again. He was apprehended and brought to trial in 1849. The *New York Herald* nicknamed him "the confidence man." The term stuck—not only to Thompson, but to all who practiced similar crimes of deceit. Thompson's exploits provided the inspiration for Herman Melville's 1857 novel *The Confidence-Man*.

Who is Walter Mitty?

Walter Mitty is a fictional character in James Thurber's short story, "The Secret Life of Walter Mitty." Published in the *New Yorker* in 1939, Mitty was a timid, meek man mercilessly henpecked by a nagging wife. He escapes his existence by daydreaming about various adventurous and triumphant exploits—he is a brilliant surgeon, gallant pilot, and courageous naval commander, among others. Thurber's work was made into a movie in 1947 starring Danny Kaye.

This story has maintained its popularity over the years, a point of identification for many individuals no doubt. The name *Walter Mitty* has become part of the American vocabulary to describe a meek, unadventurous person with secret and unfulfilled ambitions of greatness, courage, or fame.

Visit www.geocities.com/SoHo/Cafe/6821/thurber.html to read "The Secret Life of Walter Mitty" in its entirety.

4

Holidays and Special Occasions

What is Kwanzaa?

Kwanzaa is a Pan-African celebration that focuses on the traditional African values of family, community, and culture. It is a cultural holiday, not a religious one; it does not take the place of Christmas or any other religious practice or observance. The word *Kwanzaa* means "first fruits of the harvest." It is a time of reaffirming cultural connections, recommitting to African ideals, and giving respect and gratitude to one's ancestors.

Kwanzaa is celebrated from December 26 through January 1. It is based on *Nguzo Saba* (the seven guiding principles), with one principle focused on each day of Kwanza—unity, self-determination, collective work and responsibility, cooperative economics, purpose, creativity, and faith/honoring of traditions.

What is the meaning of the word *Christmas*?

Many scholars agree that the origin of the word *Christmas* is derived from the Old English *Cristes Maesse*—the Mass of Christ. The word *Christ* is likely from the Middle and Old English *Crist,* meaning the "anointed one" or "the Lord's anointed" (this in turn likely borrowed from the Latin *Christus* and Greek *Christos*, both translating as "anointed one"). *Maesse* was used to signify a festival, feast day, or mass.

The majority of Christians celebrate the birth of Christ on December 25, although Christmas is celebrated on January 7 in Coptic, Jerusalem, Russian, Serbian, and Georgian Orthodox churches. As an interesting aside, many lament the use of the word *Xmas* as they believe that it "takes the Christ out of Christmas." However, some researchers believe the X signifies the Greek letter *Chi*, which is the first letter of Christ as spelled in Greek (*Christos* = Χριστός).

What is Hogmanay?

Although welcoming of the New Year is celebrated in many ways throughout the world, the Scots have their own set of customs associated with this event called Hogmanay (hahg-muh-*nay*). Its official date is December 31, but celebrations may continue through January 2. Due in large part to the Protestant Reformation, Christmas in Scotland from the 17th century to the 1950s or 1960s was observed exclusively as a religious event and was essentially devoid of the feasting, celebrating, and gift giving that many cultures associate with Christmas. In Scotland, most of this merriment is reserved for Hogmanay! Over the years, many national and local customs have diminished or disappeared due to the major, all-night celebrations in Glasgow, Edinburgh, Aberdeen, and Dundee. However, several of the most interesting customs have persisted in varying degrees and are associated with renewal and starting a new year with a "clean slate":

- *Cleaning the house:* It is customary to thoroughly clean one's house (called "redding") on December 31. This includes sweeping the ashes from the fireplace. The last ashes of the old year are believed to *show* (much like "reading" tea leaves) what to expect in the coming year.
- *First footing:* At the stroke of midnight, bells are rung to welcome the New Year. Immediately after the bells have tolled, neighbors and friends are expected to visit to wish one another a happy and good new year. The "first foot" is the first visitor. Tradition favors a tall, dark, and handsome male to serve in this role, perhaps because a blond visitor was reminiscent of Viking visitations of yesteryear—which usually meant trouble! Women and redheads are also considered bad luck as a first foot. First foots are expected to bring a symbolic gift (called handselling) of a lump of coal to signify a warm

and safe home or shortbread to promote a full pantry for the coming year.

* *Song:* The singing of Robert Burns's "Auld Lang Syne" is accompanied by fireworks, the burning of a fireball (especially in rural areas due to extended hours of darkness), and/or toasting, customs adopted by many other countries as well.

Are St. Nicholas and Santa Claus the same person?

Yes—and no. The origin of the man we have come to know as Santa Claus began with a boy named Nicholas who was born around AD 280 in what is now Turkey. The orphaned son of wealthy parents, Nicholas is said to have used his inheritance to aid the poor, sick, and needy. He was appointed bishop of Myra and became known for his generosity, love of children, and his interest and concern for sailors and their ships. The anniversary of his death, December 6, came to be known as St. Nicholas Day, a feast day of celebration and good tidings which is still widely celebrated in Europe by gift giving and assorted merrymaking!

Celebrations related to St. Nicholas came to America via the colonists, notably the Dutch. In particular, John Pintard founded the New York Historical Society in 1804 and promoted St. Nicholas as the patron saint of the society and of New York City. Washington Irving, author of "The Legend of Sleepy Hollow" and "Rip Van Winkle" (among others), was a member of the society and frequently referenced a jolly St. Nicholas character in his writings. Greatly influenced by Irving's portrayal, Clement Clark Moore, a professor, religious scholar, and author, wrote a Christmas poem entitled "A Visit from St. Nicholas" in 1842. Wildly popular, this work became known as "The Night before Christmas." In 1881, Thomas Nast, renowned political cartoonist, reinforced this image of St. Nicholas in his regular cartoon features in *Harper's Weekly* by depicting St. Nicholas as a white-bearded, plump, elflike, pipe-smoking character. Nast portrayed him with reindeer, a bright red fur-trimmed suit, and a North Pole workshop. Also, St. Nicholas's name began to evolve to more closely resemble the German *Sankt Niklaus* and the Dutch *Sinter Klaas*.

Ironically, it was the Coca-Cola Company with its advertising campaign of the 1930s that added the finishing touch to what we believe Santa Claus does or should look like. Therefore, the secular Santa Claus as we know him today is often called St. Nick and clearly has his roots in the sacred and saintly St. Nicholas.

For more information, visit www.stnicholascenter.org or www.historychannel.com.

What are some traditions observed to bring in the new year?

The ancient Babylonians, Egyptians, and Romans were the first cultures known to celebrate the start of a new year, usually associated with the growing season. Historically, traditions developed around what was done or eaten on the first day of the new year as it was believed that this affected one's luck, health, and prosperity during the year. Most customs and traditions today focus on symbolizing a fresh start or new beginnings. Contemporary Western cultures typically consider January 1 as New Year's Day. Various customs and traditions are observed to welcome the new year, although these can differ greatly from region to region in a country or even from family to family.

In Scotland, for example, the new year (called Hogmanay) may be observed by rolling lighted barrels of tar through the streets of the village, signifying the destruction of the old year. Another custom in the British Isles is called "first footing" and involves the belief that the first guest in the home in the new year will bring good or bad luck to the household. The "preferred" guest is a dark-haired man bearing a gift. The singing of "Auld Lang Syne" at midnight, another Scottish custom, is popular in many countries now.

In Canada, many customs are similar to those in America. However, one tradition deserves special notice: the Vancouver Polar Bear Swim Club. Starting in 1920 with 10 swimmers, the event now attracts approximately 2,000 entrants! These motivated swimmers plunge into the frigid waters of English Bay competing in various events.

Many Americans attend parties or gatherings to greet the new year. Midnight is often accompanied by toasting, singing, and other forms of merriment. Due to some celebrations becoming a bit too wild and unsafe, Boston started an alcohol-free First Night celebration in 1976 to provide an arts-related alternative to the usual revelry. Approximately 220 cities have followed suit. Other people prefer to enjoy a quiet evening at home awaiting the countdown and "ball drop" in New York City's Times Square. New Year's Day is often celebrated by watching football or parades.

How was Father's Day started?

Most sources credit Mrs. Sonora Smart Dodd of Spokane, Washington, for starting the celebration of Father's Day. Inspired by a Mother's Day sermon in 1909, she wanted to honor her own father, William Smart, who had raised six children as a single parent. His wife (Sonora's mother) died in childbirth bearing their sixth child. The first Father's Day was celebrated on June 19, 1910, in Spokane. Father's Day grew in popularity and was observed in many communities across America during the next decade. Although President Calvin Coolidge declared his support for national recognition of

Father's Day, it was not until 1966 that President Lyndon Johnson signed a presidential proclamation citing the third Sunday in June as Father's Day, followed in 1972 by President Richard Nixon establishing the day as a permanent national observance.

How was Mother's Day started?

In America, the first efforts to officially honor mothers were initiated in 1872 by Julia Ward Howe, author of the lyrics for the "Battle Hymn of the Republic." She organized Mother's Day meetings in Boston to promote peace and harmony. It is Miss Anna Jarvis of Philadelphia, a native of West Virginia, however, who is widely credited with triggering a movement to establish an official day to honor mothers. In 1910, West Virginia became the first state (as a whole) to celebrate Mother's Day, followed by almost every other state the next year. President Woodrow Wilson designated the second Sunday in May as a national holiday in 1914. Mother's Day has flourished ever since in the United States and is celebrated in many other countries throughout the world in varying fashions.

Interestingly, when Anna Jarvis died in 1948, she was a woman filled with anger and regret at having established Mother's Day. She thought the day had become an occasion of greed, profit, and commercialization—not what she had intended. Never a mother herself, she was arrested for disturbing the peace at a Mother's Day activity and had filed suit to stop a Mother's Day festival in 1923.

Why is January 1 the first day of the year?

Julius Caesar, in an attempt to bring a higher degree of order and organization to an expanding Roman Empire, abolished previous calendars and established a calendar based on the earth's

113

movement in relation to the sun. Caesar wanted to establish the first day of the new year on the date of the spring equinox or the winter solstice. The Roman Senate, however, was accustomed to taking office on January 1 and wanted that date to prevail. Caesar conceded the point and January 1 was established as the first day of the new year. Ignoring Caesar's calendar (known as the Julian calendar today), other countries and/or cultures continued to use March 1, March 25, December 25, or other dates based on their own ecclesiastical, civil, or liturgical needs. The Julian calendar, although a remarkable achievement in its time, was flawed.

Pope Gregory XIII in his papal bull of February 1582 (*Inter Gravissimas*) called for reforms to improve the calendar in general, especially as it pertained to leap years and the determination of Easter. January 1, not mentioned in the bull, remained the first day of the new year. Countries throughout the world adopted Pope Gregory's calendar (now called the Gregorian calendar) at their own pace, some not until the early 20th century! An estimated 40 calendars are in use throughout the world today, many used for religious purposes only. However, the Gregorian calendar with a new year's date of January 1 is the most widely used.

To learn more about calendars, visit http://serendipity .magnet.ch.

What is Hanukkah?

Hanukkah, sometimes spelled Chanukah, is a Jewish holiday celebrating the Hebrew victory (about 2,300 years ago) over Antiochus, the Greek king of Syria, who had commanded that all subjects worship Greek gods and idols. During this time, learning Hebrew was forbidden. In defiance, Jewish children continued to study, quickly hiding their scrolls and pretending to play dreidel (also, dreydel), a game featuring a four-sided top, when Syrian authorities approached. The dreidel is still a popular Hanukkah game today. Understandably, the outlawing of Judaism angered the Jews who, under the direction and/or influence of Judas Maccabeus, fought a three-year war to restore the right to worship as they wished. Although out-manned and out-weaponed, the Jews were victorious. The victory itself was remarkable, but the true miracle occurred upon the completion of the cleansing of the Holy Temple of Jerusalem. Seeking to rededicate the temple by lighting the temple's menorah, only a small flask of consecrated oil could be found—enough to last for only one day's light. Astonishingly, the oil lasted for eight days, long enough to secure more oil to keep the flame burning.

In Hebrew, Hanukkah means "dedication." Hanukkah is also referred to as "The Festival of Lights." It is celebrated for eight days beginning on the 25th day of Kislev on the Hebrew calendar. This parallels November/December on the western or Gregorian calendar. The dates of Hanukkah vary from year to year within this two-month time frame.

The most important and sacred Hanukkah ritual involves lighting the candles of the menorah, a special candelabrum with nine "branches." Accompanied by special blessings, one candle is lit each night (in addition to the middle and tallest candle, the Shamash, meaning "servant candle" (used to light the other candles). By the end of the eight-day holiday, all of the candles are lit. Other traditions celebrated by Jewish families at Hanukkah may include gift giving, games, home decorations, and the preparation of special foods, notably latkes (potato pancakes) and *sufganiyot* (jelly doughnuts).

How did the celebration of Halloween begin?

Historical accounts of the origins and practice of Halloween vary widely and there is as much misinformation as information regarding this topic. However, despite this, it is believed that the origins of Halloween date back to at least 700 BC. The Druids celebrated the end of the harvest season on November 1. This Celtic festival was known as Samhain (sow "rhymes with cow" -win). This was a pagan event that, in time, was given somewhat of a Christian reinterpretation as honoring the dead (as All Hallows' Day, Hallow Eve, All Souls' Day, and All Hallowed Souls). The Eve of All Hallows generalized into Hallow Eve, then Hallow E'en. Various traditions evolved in different countries over the centuries. Some involved animal and crop sacrifices. In some areas it became customary to leave food on the doorstep in order to appease hungry spirits or to attract the spirits of dead loved ones. In other areas, it became a tradition for people to visit their neighbors to solicit contributions of food for a town feast. Some people wore masks or dressed as ghosts or witches as they believed that doing so prevented undesirable spirits from recognizing them as humans. Certain customs were brought to America by European immigrants and endure today in the adapted forms of dressing in costume and offering candy on Halloween.

Halloween is observed primarily in the United States, the United Kingdom, Ireland, and Canada. It is a somewhat controversial occasion. Most people do not associate pagan or religious connotations with Halloween and consider it to be a strictly secular occasion focused on harmless fun. However, others decidedly object to the darker emphasis on death, the occult, and/or elements of evil and choose to not celebrate or participate in Halloween in any way.

What is the origin of Groundhog Day?

The distinctly North American celebration of Groundhog Day has its roots in the early Roman observance of the Festival of Februa where it was believed that the hedgehog emerged from its den to predict the remaining length of winter. During the Roman conquest of certain European countries, these beliefs were likely passed along and became associated with Candlemas (also known as the Purification of the Blessed Virgin) on February 2, when the clergy blessed candles for use in the church and homes. Coincidentally, the Germans studied the hibernation habits of certain animals, notably bears, badgers, and hedgehogs, in order to formulate possible correlations and predictions regarding how long the winter weather would continue. This reinforced the secular association of these animals with Candlemas.

When Germans settled in Pennsylvania in the 1700s and 1800s, they brought the traditions of Candlemas with them. As groundhogs were available in such great abundance in Pennsylvania, groundhogs (also called woodchucks and whistle pigs) became the animal of choice for the tradition of weather prognostication. The earliest reference to Groundhog Day in Pennsylvania is at the Historical Society of Berks County in Reading, Pennsylvania, in the diary of storekeeper James Morris, dated February 4, 1841. The first official celebration of Groundhog Day, however, was held on February 2, 1886, in Punxsutawney, Pennsylvania, as proclaimed in the local newspaper, the *Punxsutawney Spirit*. The groundhog was dubbed "Punxsutawney Phil." The first trip to Gobbler's Knob, a wooded hill about two miles from town, was made the following year. Although Phil lives in climate-controlled quarters in Punxsutawney, every year he is taken to Gobbler's Knob for Groundhog Day where he is pulled from his heated burrow to prognosticate the remaining duration of winter.

Why do people kiss under mistletoe?

It is believed that Roman, Scandinavian, and English connections with mistletoe influenced the contemporary custom of kissing under the mistletoe. Before the birth of Christ, the Celtic Druids in England viewed mistletoe as a sign of peace, goodwill, and power against witches and other evil spirits. They used it decoratively, spiritually, and medicinally. Because of its association with Druid paganism, many early Christian churches banned its use, recommending the substitution of holly it its place. The Scandinavians associated mistletoe with Frigga, their goddess of beauty and love. The ancient Romans, during their festival of Saturnalia, included kissing under a sprig of mistletoe as part of their marriage rites.

The 18th-century English credited mistletoe with healing powers and created the "kissing ball," a spherical arrangement made of mistletoe, ribbons, and greenery hung from a ceiling or doorway. Reportedly, as kissing balls became more popular, proper etiquette was devised to keep the kissing under control. The gentleman was to pluck a berry from the mistletoe after each kiss. When the sprig ran out of berries, the kissing was to cease. No doubt, sprigs with abundant berries were highly prized! This rule of etiquette is little known and rarely observed in modern times.

Kissing under a sprig or ball of mistletoe has become a widespread holiday custom throughout the world, notably in Europe, America, Australia, Canada, and New Zealand. Typically considered a simple and harmless custom of merriment in the United States, some cultures consider kissing under the mistletoe to signify a binding proposal of marriage.

Mistletoe (*Viscum alba* and other species) is a semiparasitic plant. It gets its water and nutrients by sending roots down into the branches of its host plant. Mistletoe grows on a variety of trees and shrubs throughout the world, notably Europe and areas of North America. A heavy infestation of mistletoe can stunt, deform, weaken, and, in rare cases, kill its host. Mistletoe is used today in medical research and for holiday decorations. Gathering mistletoe can be tricky as much of it grows in the top of tall trees. Fortunately, mistletoe is grown and harvested commercially in Texas, Oklahoma, New Mexico, and other states.

Caution: Mistletoe leaves and berries are toxic and should be kept away from children and pets.

Why do graduates wear caps and gowns?

Academic garb dates back to 12th- and 13th-century Europe. Scholars and clerics (often one and the same) wore robes and caps daily to signify their social and/or professional status and probably for the more practical reason of better insulating themselves from the damp, cold buildings of the time. As church and state affairs became more separated, so did their manner of attire.

The mortarboard descended from the biretta, a square cap featuring three ridges or peaks, originally worn by clerics, academics, and others of higher social status. The biretta, although modified over time, was maintained by clerics. Academic headwear, especially influenced by academic dress codes established at Oxford and Cambridge in England, modified into a flatter tam or what we call

a "mortarboard" today, presumably named after the square tool (mortarboard) used by masons to carry or hold mortar.

In America, students at many colleges wore caps and gowns to class on a daily basis until around the time of the Civil War. The style, color, and other features of academic garb varied dramatically from school to school. Due to this, the American Council on Education convened in 1895 to standardize and govern issues regarding sleeve designs, colors, hoods, caps, tassels, and cords associated with academic regalia for the degree received. The council has made various revisions to its code over the years. Details are available at www.acenet.edu/faq/costume_code.html.

What are frankincense and myrrh?

Christians, as well as those of other religions, are familiar with the story of the birth of Jesus. Part of the story involves the coming of the wise men to see the baby Jesus. They brought with them three gifts—gold, frankincense, and myrrh. At that time, frankincense and myrrh were highly prized luxury items and were considered to be as valuable as precious metals or gems. Frankincense was believed to symbolize sacrifice or divinity; myrrh was a symbol of healing and "suffering love." Both were used throughout the ancient world to make ceremonial incense and anointing oil, medicinal products, perfuming or deodorizing products, and in balms used to prepare bodies for burial. They were used for both religious and civil purposes in a pure state or mixed with other spices or botanicals to create different aromas for different uses.

Frankincense and myrrh are both resins (dried sap) from certain trees or shrubs, *Boswellia* (frankincense) and *Commiphora* (myrrh). Typically, the bark was cut to allow the sap to ooze out. After the sap dried, it was collected. Both resins are still used today, primarily as incense, aromatics, and for some medicinal uses.

How is the date for Easter decided?

Easter Sunday is the day when Christians throughout the world celebrate Christ's resurrection. Essentially, following the Gregorian calendar (today's standard international calendar for civil use), Easter is observed on the first Sunday following the first ecclesiastical full moon (somewhat different from the astronomical full-moon cycle) that occurs immediately after the vernal equinox (March 21). This particular full moon is called the *paschal* (*pas*-kuhl) full moon. Using this method, Easter occurs on or between March 22 and April 25. Calendars and methods of calculation have varied throughout the centuries resulting in some Christian groups, particularly Eastern Orthodox Christian churches, often celebrating Easter on a different Sunday.

The English name *Easter* is derived from *Eastre* (sometimes *Eostre* or *Ostara*), the Anglo-Saxon goddess of spring, in whose honor a festival was held annually to celebrate the vernal equinox.

Why is Thanksgiving celebrated on the fourth Thursday in November?

The first observance of Thanksgiving in America was a religious event held in 1619 at Berkeley Plantation in Virginia. However, feasting was not associated with this event, so the first true Thanksgiving is generally credited to the Plymouth Pilgrims in 1621 and their celebration of a bountiful harvest. After that, Thanksgiving was celebrated sporadically, although some states declared official days of giving thanks.

In 1863 Abraham Lincoln established "a day for thanksgiving and prayer," to be observed on the *last* Thursday of November, due in large measure to the encouragement (some say assertive lobbying campaign) of Sarah Josepha Hale. Hale was the editor of *Godey's Lady's Book* and was a crusader for equal educational opportunities for girls and daycare for children of working mothers. A prolific writer, she is perhaps best known for writing the words to the famed children's nursery rhyme "Mary Had a Little Lamb."

In 1939, President Franklin D. Roosevelt, in the annual presidential Thanksgiving Proclamation, set the holiday on the *next-to-last* Thursday of November. It proved to be an unpopular change. In 1941, Congress set the date as the *fourth* Thursday in November—whether or not it was the last or next-to-last Thursday of the month—and established it as a federal holiday.

Other countries celebrate Thanksgiving or harvest festivals during the autumn season, including Japan, South Korea, Laos, Liberia, and Canada.

Who was St. Valentine?

Valentine's Day is a popular occasion devoted to the celebration or pursuit of love. Typically marked by the giving of cards, candy, flowers, or other tokens of affection, Valentine's Day as we know it today was born of religious and pagan roots. Cloaked in a degree of uncertainty, a common version of how Valentine's Day originated begins with a fifth-century Roman celebration to honor two deities, Juno and Lupercus. Part of these mid-February celebrations involved the custom of conducting a lottery where a young man drew the name of an unmarried girl out of a container. The girl selected became his companion for a period of time, sometimes for the entire year. Appalled by this practice, early Christian leaders are said to have altered the custom by having the names of saints placed in the container to be selected by both young men and women with the idea that the name drawn would serve as a model to emulate for the upcoming year. (You can imagine how the young men of Rome must have reacted to this rule change!)

Although several saints named "Valentine" (all martyred), are recognized by the Catholic Church, a likely candidate to continue with this legend involves Valentine, a priest who served during the third century in Rome. During this same time, Emperor Claudius II believed that unmarried men made the best soldiers and decreed against marriage for young men of military age. Valentine, sympathetic to the young men's plight, secretly married those who came to him asking to be married despite the prohibition. Imprisoned for this defiance and for refusing to renounce his faith, Valentine is said to have fallen in love with the jailer's blind daughter. His faith and his great love for her miraculously cured her blindness. He is also credited with signing his last letter to her "From your Valentine," before his beating and beheading (coincidentally on February 14, AD 270). In AD 496, Valentine was named as the patron saint of lovers to replace the pagan Juno and Lupercus. The occasion, re-named St. Valentine's Day, was celebrated on February 14.

Although dropped from the Catholic calendar of feasts by Pope Paul VI in 1969, Valentine's Day is still an extremely popular occasion for sweethearts of all ages.

5

Humanities and Culture

Why do men's suits have buttons on the backs of their sleeves?

As is true of many conventions of fashion, historical dress influences contemporary style even after the original function has long disappeared. For example, most men's suits have two, three, or four buttons on each sleeve. Most are decorative, not functional. Some jackets even feature faux buttonholes stitched into the fabric to simulate working buttons and/or vents that are sewn to make the sleeve cuff appear to be functional. Buttons are often simply sewn on the cuff area of jacket sleeves without the sartorial details of vents or buttonhole stitching. Nonworking sleeve buttons probably resulted from the desire to keep the look of finely tailored clothing without the associated cost. Working sleeve buttons are typically found on high-end men's suit jackets—although not always.

Sleeves with working buttons are called "surgeon's cuffs." Gentlemen of yesteryear rarely removed their jackets in public as doing so was deemed socially inappropriate. Furthermore, the chilliness of most dwellings and commercial establishments encouraged the wearing of layers of clothing for warmth. Surgeons, by necessity, had the need to roll up their sleeves to accomplish various medical procedures, all the while keeping their coats on. Buttoned sleeves facilitated this need. Also, riding coats of the 18th century and military garb of the 19th century often had sleeve cuffs that folded back and buttoned into place. Undoubtedly, all of these garments influenced the appearance of modern menswear.

What is Sudoku?

Sudoku (sue-*doh*-koo) is a logic-based number puzzle. The word *Sudoku* is Japanese for "numbers singly." It is a logic-based brain-teaser whose popularity has spread internationally. It was created in 1979 by Howard Garns, a freelance puzzle designer, and was published by Dell with the name "Number Place." In the mid-1980s, the game was published by Nikoli, a Japanese publisher that specializes in logic puzzles. Nikoli renamed the game to the now familiar Sudoku. Although typically played with numbers, letters, shapes, or colors can be used as long as the rules of the game are followed. Difficulty levels vary, ranging from Sudoku for kids to Sudoku for those desiring a significant and difficult challenge.

8	5	4	3	1	6	9	2	7
7	6	2	8	5	9	4	1	3
1	3	9	2	7	4	8	6	5
3	9	1	4	8	5	2	7	6
2	8	7	9	6	1	5	3	4
6	4	5	7	2	3	1	9	8
4	7	6	1	9	8	3	5	2
9	2	8	5	3	7	6	4	1
5	1	3	6	4	2	7	8	9

A Sudoku puzzle is similar to a crossword puzzle in that it features a grid of cells. Typically, there are 81 cells arranged in nine regions (also called blocks or boxes); each region is composed of nine cells in a 3-by-3 arrangement. There are three regions in three rows to constitute the puzzle. Selected cells contain numbers at the start of the game; these are called *givens* or *clues*. The object of the game is to fill in all of the cells so that every row, every column, and every 3-by-3 region contains the digits 1 through 9 as in the completed example provided; the bold numbers are the givens.

Sudoku puzzles may be purchased in most bookstores and are available (some free, some for a fee) online.

In college athletics, what is the difference between a redshirt freshman and a true freshman?

In accordance with the NCAA (National Collegiate Athletic Association), a student athlete may only play four seasons in a given sport. A true freshman is exactly what it sounds like—a player in a sport during his or her first year in college classes. However, a player may miss or skip his or her freshman year of play due to injury, academic difficulties, or a coach's decision to not play a player. Players designated as *redshirted* are still in college and may practice with the team, but they *do not compete* against outside competition in the sport's season for the entire academic year. If the freshman is redshirted, barring any other disqualifiers, the athlete is still eligible to play four full seasons in addition to the redshirt period.

How did the bikini get its name?

The bikini swimsuit made its debut in 1947. It was the skimpy fashion creation of Parisian engineer Louis Reard based on the design of Jacques Heim. Coincidentally, the United States chose the Bikini

Atoll in the Ralik chain of the Marshall Islands in the Pacific Ocean to conduct nuclear tests beginning in 1946. Because the new swimwear caused such an atomic-like burst of attention and interest from many, particularly men, the name *bikini* seemed appropriate and stuck.

At the beginning, designers found it difficult to find women even willing to model this daring swimsuit. In America the 1960 song by Brian Hyland, "Itsy Bitsy Teenie Weenie Yellow Polka Dot Bikini," followed by a spate of beach-oriented teen movies resulted in more social acceptance of the garment and its continuing popularity even today.

What is a mentor?

A mentor is someone who guides, helps, or otherwise advises another person, usually over an extended period of time. A mentor, often older than the mentee, can be almost anyone—a parent, teacher, counselor, or a coworker. Formal mentoring programs are often a part of the induction of new teachers or businesspersons in their field; newcomers are paired with a wise, more experienced employee in order to quickly and effectively "learn the ropes."

In Homer's *Odyssey*, Mentor (man's name) is the trusted elderly friend of Odysseus who tutors and gives advice to Odysseus' son, Telemachus. Athena, goddess of wisdom, often disguised herself as Mentor and, as such, accompanied Telemachus on his search for his father upon the fall of Troy.

What is the difference between billiards and pool?

Billiards or billiardlike games have been played since the 14th century in Europe and China, although the form we know today evolved around 1800 from an outdoor stick and ball game. Billiards typically refers to one of many games that are played on a rectangular, bumpered or raised-edge, cloth-covered table. Game gear includes a cue stick and a set of balls, usually made of composition material. Three basic types of billiards are played: carom billiards, pocket billiards (usually called pool), and snooker. The object of billiard games in general is to strike or pocket balls. There are many variations of billiards involving the number or placement of balls, using pockets or not, the size of the pockets, scoring considerations, and boundaries on the table.

In general, the term *billiards* refers to games played on tables that have no pockets and scoring involves contact being made with certain balls. *Pool* typically refers to pocket billiard games. Pool games may include eight ball, nine ball, or straight pool. All forms of billiards are played for entertainment and often for money.

Many people use the terms *billiards* (from the French *billiart*, meaning stick) and *pool* interchangeably. The term *pool* may originate from its association with gambling on horse races. These places were called *poolrooms*; people "pooled" their money to determine the odds on the horses. Billiard tables were often available in these places, hence the association in name. Another school of thought suggests that the name *pool* came from the French slang *poule*, referring to the practice of betting on billiard games by putting money in a pot.

What is the significance of the Rosetta stone?

The Rosetta stone was found by Napoleon's troops in the Egyptian town of Rosetta (now called Rashid) in 1799. It provided the key to the modern understanding and translating of ancient Egyptian hieroglyphics. The Rosetta stone, which dates back to 196 BC, is engraved with passages that praise King Ptolemy V and describe his coronation. The inscription is written three times in different languages—once in hieroglyphic (used by ancient Egyptians for priestly purposes), once in demotic (Egyptian language for everyday use), and once in Greek (used by Greeks and other eastern Europeans). Demotic and Greek were known languages in the 19th century. Englishman Thomas Young deciphered many hieroglyphic proper nouns (such as places and names), and Frenchman Jean-François Champollion worked to compare the known to the unknown. From this, scientists were able to use the Rosetta stone as a starting point to translate most of the inscriptions on Egyptian monuments and artifacts. The Rosetta stone measures 3 feet, 9 inches high; 2 feet, 4.5 inches wide; and 11 inches thick, and it is exhibited in the British Museum in London.

Used as a metaphor, *Rosetta stone* refers to a key to the understanding or decoding of something of great importance. For example:

* Gene mapping research may provide the Rosetta stone to curing cancer.

In Chinese philosophy, what do yin and yang mean?

As early as the fourth century BC, Chinese philosophers referred to natural phenomena as *yin* (that which is shaded) and *yang* (that which is sunny). Over time, the Chinese study of the physical universe, called *cosmology*, developed to include all elements of time and space. Yin, considered female or feminine, represents all things dark, negative, moist, or receptive. Yang, considered male or masculine, represents all things light, positive, dry, and active. Yin and yang came to represent all things opposite yet complementary, co-existing in harmony and, in fact, containing parts of each other, therefore being inseparable. The interaction of yin and yang together is thought to bring harmony and balance to the natural world.

Yin and yang are symbolized as a circle of intertwined dark and light with a dot of the opposing color embedded in each half.

What is the Heisman Trophy?

The Heisman Trophy is named after John W. Heisman, a coach, sportswriter, and lifelong football enthusiast. He considered his most notable achievement to be his work to legalize the forward pass. In "retirement," Heisman was named the first athletic director of the Downtown Athletic Club (DAC) of New York City, during which time he established the Touchdown Club of New York and the National Football Coaches Association. It was at this time that Heisman formulated the procedure to honor the best college football player in the country (originally east of the Mississippi River); the first award, called the Downtown Athletic Club Award, was given to Jay Berwanger of the University of Chicago in 1935. Too large for his family's mantel, he gave it to his Aunt Gussie, who used the trophy as a doorstop. Heisman died of pneumonia before the next year's award could be given. By a unanimous vote, DAC officials changed the name of the award to the Heisman Memorial Trophy in his honor. Since 1968, two awards are presented per year—one to the player and one to the school he represents.

The bronze trophy itself was designed by the noted sculptor Frank Eliscu. The model he used was Ed Smith, a leading player on the 1934 New York University football team. It is said that Smith was unaware of this distinction until 50 years later! Ironically, Eliscu used a newspaper photograph of Jay Berwanger to provide certain details for the sculpture.

To learn more about the Heisman Trophy, visit www.heisman
.com.

What is a clique?

A clique ("click") is typically a small group of people whose members tend to have many things in common, like to associate with each other, and generally do not welcome others into the group. *Clique* is a word that is almost always used in a negative or unflattering sense. For example:

- There is a clique of sixth-grade girls that is unkind to the other girls in the class.
- I did not join the bridge club because it seemed to be formed of very cliquey people.
- The women's department at my favorite store seems to be staffed by a snooty clique of employees.

Interestingly, *clique* is also a term used in mathematics, technology, and other fields, although with very different meanings.

How did the painting *Whistler's Mother* get its name?

The name of this well-known work of art is actually *Arrangement in Grey and Black No. 1: The Painter's Mother*. It has, however, become universally known as *Whistler's Mother*. This painting is the work of the American-born artist, James McNeill Whistler (1834–1903) and was, indeed, posed for in 1871 by Anna McNeil Whistler, the artist's mother. The painting now hangs in the Musée d'Orsay in Paris.

It is said that Mrs. Whistler was a stand-in for a model who became ill and could not pose. Whistler's original vision was to have the model standing, but Mrs. Whistler is said to have been unable to stand for long periods of time—hence, she posed sitting. Offended that his painting was almost rejected by the 104th Exhibition of the Royal Academy of Art in London, where he and his mother were living at the time, he pawned the painting. Purchased by the Musée du Luxembourg, its display brought Whistler acclaim and attracted much appreciated patronage. Whistler was a prolific artist and influenced many other artists of the day.

Whistler was an early proponent of *ars gratia artis* (art for art's sake). He was puzzled as to why anyone would care that the subject was his mother. He believed that the work should simply be appreciated for its intrinsic value. Interestingly, *Whistler's Mother* has become a symbol for motherhood and maternal affection and devotion.

What is the Donner Pass?

The Donner Pass is located in the northern Sierra Nevada in eastern California, near Lake Tahoe. It, as well as Donner Lake, is named after the Donner family, who played a significant role in one of American history's most horrific pioneer tragedies. As economic opportunities in the eastern states became fewer and disease and poor sanitation became more rampant, many families in the mid-19th century headed west in hopes of a better life. Others traveled simply for the adventure. One expedition was formed by the Donner and Reed families from Illinois and Iowa; they began their journey in covered wagons in the summer of 1846. Upon reaching the ranges of the Sierra Nevada, they received conflicting advice about whether to take the known, previously traveled route or a newly discovered pass across the mountains. Many in the party decided to travel the known route and left in that direction; the Donner and Reed families along with other travelers chose the newer route and set out to reach California as quickly as possible. George Donner was chosen as wagon master, and the group at this point became known as the Donner party.

As the Donner party pressed on, a combination of hunger, the loss of oxen and cattle, and difficult terrain took its toll. In addition, word came that the route they were taking was impassable. Finding an alternate route cost them an additional 125 miles. The party was exhausted and fractious. Fighting was common. James Reed killed a man in self-defense and was banished from the group. On October 31, when the group was just 1,000 feet from the granite summit, snow began to fall. A decision was made to rest in preparation to cross the mountain. This was a devastating mistake. The travelers quickly became trapped by 20-foot snowdrifts. For the next four months, 87 men, women, and children huddled miserably near starvation in brush and cloth huts. Many died. The group eventually resorted to cannibalism, surviving on the flesh of the deceased.

A series of four relief parties, one led by the banished James Reed, began evacuating the 47 (sources vary in citing the actual number) survivors in February. Reed's wife and all four children survived. The entire Donner family died, with the exception of one child.

For additional information, visit www.tahoe.com/article/99999999/COMMUNITY06/11113006.

On the one dollar bill, what does the pyramid represent?

Looking at the back of a dollar bill, you can see two circles—one with a pyramid and the other with an eagle. These are the back (reverse) and front (obverse) sides of the Great Seal of the United States. According to the Department of State's website (www.state.gov), the pyramid signifies strength and endurance. The eye at the top of the pyramid, surrounded in a shining glory, in combination with the Latin motto, *ANNUIT COEPTIS*, symbolizes and translates as "He (God) has favored our undertakings." This implies divine favor toward American causes or endeavors. The Roman numerals at the base of the pyramid (MDCCLXXVI) translate to 1776, the year of the signing of the Declaration of Independence. The phrase on the banner under the pyramid, *NOVUS ORDO SECLORUM*, means "a new order of the ages" (the beginning of a new era in 1776).

In the legal sense, what is graft?

The word *graft* is an Americanism that refers to a form of corruption, often political, where one gains money, position, or some other type of benefit by unfair means. This can involve actual theft or simply taking advantage of one's position. The person or persons offering the money or other considerations is also guilty of graft. In other words, graft is a type of bribery and is usually illegal as well as unethical. If the corrupt individual also belongs to a professional organization (like the American Bar Association or the American Medical Association), the organization can also bring sanctions. Examples of usage are:

- The man paid thousands of dollars in graft to assure that his company was awarded the city contract.
- Billions of dollars are lost to graft and corruption every year in the world of business, yet very few people are ever held accountable.

What do the five Olympic rings represent?

The Olympic rings are a familiar sight, especially when the Olympic Games are under way. The five rings are blue, black, red, yellow, and green. They are the brainchild of Pierre de Coubertin (1863–1937), the chief architect of the revival and reestablishment of the modern Olympics in 1896. He proposed an Olympic flag displaying five interlocking circles or rings on a white background. The interlocking colored rings represent the union of the five major areas of the world (Africa, the Americas, Asia, Europe, and Oceania); the white background represents peace. Pierre de Coubertin is quoted as saying, "The six colours, including the white background, represent the colours of all the world's flags . . . this is a true international emblem." The Olympic flag was first displayed at the 1920 Olympic Games in Antwerp, Belgium.

Was Mother Goose a real person?

The name *Mother Goose* is believed to have been first used in 1650 in France. The name was seen again in Charles Perrault's fairy tales (*Tales of My Mother Goose*), published in 1697, which includes favorites such as "Cinderella" and "Little Red Riding Hood." This book was very popular and widely translated from its original French. Other references to Mother Goose exist, and in the late 18th century John Newbery (for whom the Newbery Medal is named) published *Mother Goose's Melody*. This really made Mother Goose a household name and changed the focus from fairy tales to nursery rhymes.

Over the years, many people have claimed that a woman from late 17th-century Boston named Elizabeth Goose (sometimes written as Vergoose or Vertigoose), was the true Mother Goose. According to folklore, she was a widow who married a man with 10 children and later bore six children herself. Various legends still exist, some crediting her with writing, editing, and/or publishing nursery rhymes. However, no such tome has ever been found. Others say that she simply provided an image of what we think she does (or should) look like! However, scholars have never been able to substantiate Elizabeth Goose's association with any book or image.

Perhaps the most widely known version of Mother Goose, *The Real Mother Goose*, is a collection of various rhymes published in 1916 with cover and illustrations by Blanche Fisher Wright.

What is braille?

Braille is a system used by blind or visually challenged persons to read and write. Letters and numbers are based on a system of one to six raised dots. Each raised dot has a numbered position on a braille cell.

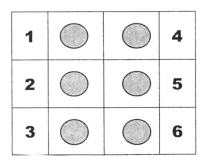

To illustrate:

Using the diagram above, the letter *A* is written by one dot in the 1 position. *B* is represented by two dots in the 1 and 2 positions. Each letter of the alphabet, numbers, and punctuation can be determined based on the number and configuration of the raised dots.

The term *braille* is taken from the name of its creator, Louis Braille (1809–1852). Braille was born in a small village near Paris. As a young boy, he was blinded accidentally in his father's harness workshop with an awl, a sharp tool used to punch holes in leather. An infection developed in his injured eye and spread to his other eye, causing total blindness. His parents sent him to a special school in Paris that specialized in teaching blind children. Teaching methods were limited at this time and young Braille became increasingly frustrated. Luckily, a former French army captain visited his school and shared his code of 12 raised dots which he called "night writing." This code was used in the military to share information at night, when speaking aloud would be dangerous, and to encode secret messages. Because of its difficulty, it was not universally used in the military. Twelve-year-old Braille, however, seized upon the idea and from it developed the braille system used today throughout the world.

Is there such a thing as a million dollar bill?

No. There are currently seven denominations of U.S. paper currency (banknotes) in circulation—$1, $2, $5, $10, $20, $50, and $100 bills. The highest-value banknote that has ever been printed by the Bureau of Engraving and Printing was the $100,000 gold certificate, series 1934. These were printed to be used in transactions between the U.S. Treasury and Federal Reserve banks. The general public never had access to these bills.

On July 6, 1785, the dollar was selected as the money unit for the United States. The name *dollar* originated from the Spanish dollar, a silver coin widely used during the Revolutionary War. According to the U.S. Bureau of Engraving and Printing, the dollar sign ($) is most likely the result of individuals drawing an *S* over the Mexican or Spanish *P* for pesos or pieces of eight.

Since 1862, the secretary of the treasury has had responsibility for the designs and portraits that are engraved on paper currency. Currency designs on U.S. bills are listed below.

Banknote	Portrait on the Front	Design on the Back
$1	George Washington	Great Seal of the United States
$2	Thomas Jefferson	Signing of the Declaration of Independence (2nd issue)
$5	Abraham Lincoln	Lincoln Memorial
$10	Alexander Hamilton	U.S. Treasury Building
$20	Andrew Jackson	White House
$50	Ulysses S. Grant	U.S. Capitol
$100	Benjamin Franklin	Independence Hall
$500*	William McKinley	Ornamental 500
$1,000*	Grover Cleveland	Ornamental 1,000
$5,000*	James Madison	Ornamental 5,000
$10,000*	Salmon P. Chase	Ornamental 10,000
$100,000*	Woodrow Wilson	Ornamental 100,000

*No longer printed, circulated, and/or for public use.

Why do outhouse doors have a crescent moon cut into them?

In colonial America, one typically either used the out-of-doors to take care of "bathroom" business, or used a chamber pot, which was emptied daily by a servant or the user of the pot. Outhouses, it is believed, were first used in Europe. They became popular in America by innkeepers who often had two outhouses for their establishments—one for male and one for female travelers. Remember, at this time in history, widespread illiteracy was the norm and America was a land of many languages. In order to prevent confusion and embarrassment, innkeepers used a sunburst (often resembling a star) for Sol, an ancient sign meaning male, and a crescent moon for Luna, an ancient symbol for women. The symbols were often cut into the doors—thus providing light and ventilation.

It is speculated that as outhouses fell into disrepair, the most unusable structures were destroyed or abandoned and the remaining outhouses were designated for women. It was believed that men could more easily "visit" the woods, whereas women would have more difficulty doing so. As time passed, the crescent moon became a universal decoration for most all outhouses. Outhouses were usually made of wood, although fancier outhouses were sometimes built and often contained two or more openings for use. This allowed the user to select the best size as it could be quite a bad experience to attempt to sit on an opening that was too large. (You get the picture!) As areas became more populated, residents often considered an outhouse to be an offensive structure to be in view of other homes, and it was common for owners to awaken in the morning to find that their outhouses were destroyed or had simply vanished!

Who invented the zipper?

Elias Howe, the inventor of the sewing machine, is believed to have been the original inventor of the zipper. He applied for a patent for his closure, but for unknown reasons, he never pursued marketing it. Almost half a century later, in 1893, Whitcomb Judson, also an inventor, sought to help a friend whose stiff back made it very difficult to fasten his shoes. Judson's "Clasp Locker" was a crude hook and eye design. Judson is credited as the inventor of the zipper because he was the first to offer it for sale. In 1913 Gideon Sundback, a Swedish-born engineer and former employee of Judson, made steps to improve and refine Judson's clasp for practical use. The result had a metal "teeth" design and was a close relative to the modern-day zipper.

It was the BF Goodrich Company that gave the clasp a boost in sales and the name *zipper*. Using Sundback's device, it became possible to fasten rubber boots with one "zip" of the hand, plus these metal fasteners made an appealing "zipping" sound.

Today, zippers are typically made of metal, plastic, or nylon and are used on luggage, clothing, sports equipment, furniture cushions, and a host of other products.

What is a governmental summit?

According to *Webster's New World College Dictionary*, a summit is a meeting of the highest level of officials, often the diplomatic heads of government. The purpose of these gatherings is to conduct face-to-face discussions usually on a specific topic, issue, or concern that in some way involves all of the countries or entities represented at the summit, and sometimes those not represented. They may be international, regional, national, or local in nature. Summits may focus on economics, politics, the environment, human rights, poverty, peace, disaster management, and other issues.

The topics of concern demand the attention and voice of authority and can even involve, for example, the presidents or prime ministers of countries. Summits can also be organized for top businesspersons, museum directors, or school officials to work on issues specific to their interests or concerns. The results of summits vary greatly. Sometimes a definitive course of action is set; on other occasions a broader understanding is sought for future consideration or action.

Who was L. Frank Baum?

L. Frank Baum was a prolific writer of books, short stories, and songs. Arguably, his most famous works were his Oz books. Baum actually wrote 14 books about Oz. He also wrote a book of Oz short stories. The original, and most well known book in the series, was written in 1900 and was titled *The Wonderful Wizard of Oz*. It spawned a Broadway musical called *The Wizard of Oz*. When the book was reissued by a different publisher (the original publisher having gone bankrupt), it was called *The New Wizard of Oz*, but the use of "New" was quickly dropped, probably due to the familiarity with the play.

Upon Baum's death in 1919, the publisher hired Ruth Plumly Thompson, a Philadelphia native, to continue penning Oz books, initially under Baum's name. She wrote 19 Oz books in all. Thompson is also known as a writer of fairy tales, fiction, and other works. In addition, other authors wrote several of the later Oz books.

The popularity of *The Wizard of Oz* reached new heights in 1939 with the release of MGM's film version, starring Judy Garland. The movie is now considered a classic and a favorite of adults and children alike.

What is a pundit?

According to *Webster's New World College Dictionary*, a pundit is "a person who has or professes to have great learning, actual or self-professed authority." This word is taken from the Hindi word *pandit* for one who is learned in Sanskrit and/or Hindu philosophy, law, and religion. Although there are many uses for the word "pundit" in various professions or areas of interest, it is probably used most often in reference to politics. A political pundit is one who is (or believes himself or herself to be) an expert, a valued source of opinion, or an informed critic of events, policies, or other areas of political life. Examples of usage are:

- ❧ Having made an A in his freshman political science course, Jack considered himself a novice pundit.
- ❧ Pundit George Stephanopoulos recently appeared as a guest on *Face the Nation*.
- ❧ The newspaper music pundit condemned the new recording before she had even heard it!

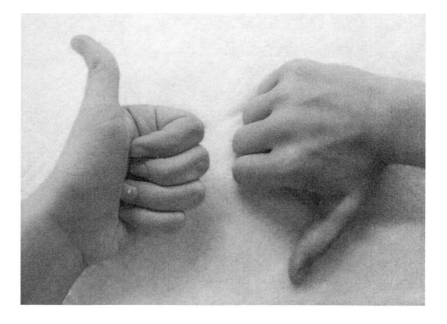

What does the "2" on pencils mean?

The pencil is perhaps the most widely used and readily available writing tool in the world. The pencil has its origins in the use of various metals, such as silver, lead, and zinc, to write on various surfaces. Despite the fact that these metals are not used in the pencils that we use today, we persist in calling them lead pencils and the material in pencils, lead.

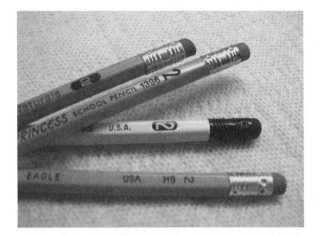

In 1564 an exceptionally pure deposit of what we today call graphite was discovered in England. Prized as an excellent writing material because it made darker marks than lead, the graphite was mined and encased in a wooden shaft for use as a pencil-like writing instrument. In time, this supply of graphite dwindled. This problem was eventually solved because it was discovered that less pure graphite, found in many places around the world, could be crushed and concentrated for use. It was not until 1795 that a Frenchman, Jacques Conté, an inventor, adventurer, artist, and officer in Napoleon's army, developed a process to mix powdered graphite with clay. When molded into rods or sticks and baked, a durable and less expensive product resulted. Conté was able to assign a "grade" to the rods based on the proportions of graphite and clay used. More clay in the mixture resulted in "lead" that was harder and made lighter, finer marks on paper. More graphite in the mixture resulted in softer "lead" that made darker, heavier marks. The

Conté process was adopted by most, if not all, pencil makers and is still used today, largely unchanged.

American manufacturers use a numbered system (#1, #2, #3, #4) to describe how hard the "lead" is. The higher the number, the harder the lead. Softer #1 pencils are often favored by artists; harder leads like #3 and #4 are often used for drafting or engineering purposes. The #2 pencil is considered to be the middle or standard grade and is used for general purposes and by schoolchildren. Other countries use their own grading systems. You may see "HB" stamped on your #2 pencils. This is the British grade that is equivalent to our #2 and stands for "hardness and blackness." You may also see the letter *F*, designating that the pencil is designed to be sharpened to a fine point. In addition, you may see other variations of numerals and letters to note hardness and blackness, especially if your pencil is of European origin.

According to the Musgrave Pencil Company (www.pencils.net/facts.cfm), 14 billion pencils are produced around the world every year; 2 billion of these are made in the United States. The average pencil will draw a line 70 miles long or write 45,000 words and can be sharpened 17 times. Erasers were not added until about 100 years ago. Many teachers opposed having them as they believed that they would encourage students to make mistakes. One average-size tree will make about 300,000 pencils. Famous authors such as Ernest Hemingway and John Steinbeck used pencils to write their books and Francis Scott Key wrote "The Star Spangled Banner" in pencil.

What is Scotland Yard?

Scotland Yard is the headquarters of the Metropolitan Police Service (MPS), the law enforcement agency responsible for policing the greater London area (London itself is policed by the City of London

Police). The MPS functions in the protection of royalty and certain government officials, countering terrorism, and a host of other law enforcement responsibilities regarding British interests at home and abroad. Officially called the New Scotland Yard, the "newness" is derived from the fact that the agency has moved twice in its history, in 1890 and 1967. Contrary to what you might think, Scotland Yard is located in London near the Houses of Parliament, not in Scotland, and is *not* responsible for any police services in Scotland. The most prevalent explanation as to how Scotland Yard got its name involves the MPS's founding in 1829 by Sir Robert Peel, a British statesman. (As a point of interest, the nickname for police-men, *bobbies,* is taken from his name.) The back of the property where the Metropolitan Police building was located opened into a courtyard that had formerly been part of a residence owned by the king of Scotland, which he and his ambassadors used when visiting London. When James VI of Scotland became the king of England *and* Scotland as James I in 1603, maintaining this residence was no longer necessary and the property was used for various governmental purposes.

When most people refer to Scotland Yard, they are thinking about a specific branch, the Criminal Investigation Department (CID). These plain clothed detectives are internationally renowned for their crime-solving skills and serve in an advisory capacity to other police departments in the country and abroad.

Who was Icarus?

According to Greek mythology, Icarus (*Ick*-a-rus) was the son of Daedalus (*Dead*-uh-lus). Daedalus was a master architect, crafts-man, and inventor. Daedalus became quite envious when he saw that his young apprentice, his nephew, was displaying skills that approached his own. Daedalus killed him and fled to the island of Crete. To simplify the story, here Daedalus worked for King Minos building a labyrinth to house the Minotaur, a half human, half bull, born to the queen. Some years later, Daedalus took part in a plot to slay the Minotaur, which resulted not only in the Minotaur's death, but in the elopement of the king's daughter with Theseus, the man who actually killed the Minotaur. King Minos was furious at the death of the Minotaur, the loss of his daughter, and at being betrayed by Daedalus. He imprisoned Daedalus and his son, Icarus, in the labyrinth.

Realizing that escape by land or sea was impossible, Daedalus built a set of wings for himself and for his son from wood, thread, wax, and feathers. He cautioned Icarus to take care not to fly too low as the dampness from the sea would make the wings too heavy to lift and not to fly too high as the heat from the sun would melt the wax that held the feathers in place. Icarus, however, was so thrilled with his newfound ability to fly and the beauty of what he was able to see, he forgot or ignored his father's advice. He flew too close to the sun. As his father had forewarned, the wax melted and Icarus fell and drowned in the sea. Daedalus successfully completed his flight to Sicily.

This story is often used today to caution children to listen to and benefit from parental advice and as a reminder for all of us, in general, to not act foolishly or imprudently.

Who was Bojangles?

Bill "Bojangles" Robinson was a renowned African American dancer on the vaudeville circuit, on Broadway, and in 14 motion pictures. Often referred to as "King of the Tap Dancers," he is perhaps most famous for his fluid, rhythmic, and complex footwork on staircases. Of particular note, he starred with Shirley Temple in four motion pictures: *The Little Colonel* (1935); *The Littlest Rebel* (1935); *Rebecca of Sunnybrook Farm* (1938); and *Just Around the Corner* (1938). He also appeared with Lena Horne in *Stormy Weather* (1943). Breaking many race barriers in his day, he was popular with both black and white audiences.

Mr. Bojangles, as he was often affectionately called, was born Luther Robinson in Richmond, Virginia, in 1878. He was orphaned as a very young boy and raised by his grandmother, a former slave. He got the nickname "Bojangles" during his childhood, but when asked, he asserted that he did not know its origin. He ran away from home at the age of nine to Washington, D.C., where he worked as a stablehand and polished his dancing skills on the streets and in taverns.

A man of many contradictions, he was as well known for his kind and likable performing personality as he was for his hot temper in his personal life. It is estimated that he earned 3 million dollars during his long career, yet he died a debtor in 1949. It is said he lived rather lavishly and was a gambler. Generous to a fault, however, he was a true humanitarian, giving to the community and needy individuals on a regular basis.

Who was Francis Bellamy?

Francis Bellamy (1855–1931) wrote the original version of the American Pledge of Allegiance. Born in New York, he later moved to Boston and served as a Baptist minister. He was considered to be a Christian Socialist, and his views and ideas often got him into hot water with his congregation. Bellamy left the ministry and got a job working for the *Youth Companion*, a popular family magazine. Later, he also became chairman of a committee of state superintendents of education in the National Education Association. As part of his duties, he organized an event to celebrate the 400-year anniversary (quadricentennial) of Christopher Columbus's arrival in the New World. Bellamy wrote the original version of the pledge and published it in the September 8, 1892, edition of the *Companion*, and sent leaflets to schools across the country so that children could recite it on Columbus Day.

The original version of the Pledge of Allegiance reads:

I pledge allegiance to my flag, and the Republic for which it stands: one nation indivisible, with liberty and justice for all.

Several revisions have taken place over the years. Bellamy added the word, "to" preceding "the Republic" in October 1892. In 1923 "my flag" was amended at the National Flag Conference to read, "the flag of the United States," as it was believed that foreign-born children and adults may be pledging their native flag, not the U.S. flag. "Of America" was added in 1924. Congress officially recognized the pledge in 1942, and in 1954 during the Eisenhower administration, it added the words "under God." In making this change, Eisenhower said, "in this way we are reaffirming the transcendence of religious faith in America's heritage and future; in this way we shall constantly strengthen those spiritual weapons which forever will be our country's most powerful resource in peace and war."

What is a babushka?

Babushka (buh-*bush*-kuh) is a term used to describe a head scarf, usually triangular in shape, worn with the ends tied under a woman's or girl's chin. This is an Americanized definition presumably generalized from the Russian word *baba*, meaning "grandmother."

As many Russians and Russian immigrants wore (and wear) this type of scarf, the term took on both meanings. In Russia, "babushka" is used as a term for one's grandmother or an older woman—not a scarf. Two examples of Russian usage are:

- ☞ My dear babushka baked tea cookies for me.
- ☞ The babushkas shop daily at the market to purchase the freshest fruits and vegetables.

Although typically called *matryoshka* dolls, Russian nesting dolls (wooden dolls where one doll layer is removed and another doll is inside, and so on) are occasionally described using the word *babushka*, and *babushka* can be used in this sense to describe a complex or "layered" event or situation, such as:

- ☞ The judge had difficulty dismantling the babushka of the defendant's version of the crime.

What is a prothonotary?

A prothonotary is an elected official who serves as clerk of the court of common pleas. He or she keeps the records of civil proceedings. All civil litigation is filed with the prothonotary including, but not limited to, unpaid debt complaints, mortgage foreclosures, liens, and family court matters. The prothonotary also signs all writs and processes, takes bail in civil proceedings, receives petitions related to roads and rights of way, and processes naturalization papers. Functions of the office vary depending on the jurisdiction or focus (religious or civil) served.

From the Latin language for "first or chief scribe," prothonotaries are found throughout history in England, in ecclesiastical law as an officer of the court of Rome, and in some states such as Delaware. The office may have had its most famous moment when President Harry S. Truman was confronted with the term and reportedly exclaimed, "what the h——is a prothonotary?"

What is anti-Semitism?

To explore this topic, it is important to understand the term "Semite." A Semite is a person who descended from Shem, the oldest of Noah's three sons, or a person who speaks a Semitic language, such as a Hebrew, Arab, or Phoenician. The word has come to refer specifically, however, to Jews. Jews are not a race of people, as is sometimes assumed, but are a people bound by their religion, culture, and history. Contemporary use of "anti-Semitism" can be traced to 1879, when it was used by Wilhelm Marr, a German journalist, who founded the Anti-Semitic League. The term is now primarily used to describe anti-Jewish attitudes, stereotypes, hostilities, prejudice, discrimination, and/or hatred, which can take the form of cruel comments; vandalism to homes and synagogues; exclusion from jobs, housing, social occasions, and other opportunities; and, in its extreme, physical attack. Anti-Semitism was clearly demonstrated during World War II in Nazi Germany as millions of Jews were interned and then exterminated in concentration camps.

In the United States, schools, churches, and the police actively work to lessen or eliminate forms of prejudice, bigotry, and hatred against *any* and *all* groups. Nationally-known organizations that combat anti-Semitism include the Anti-Defamation League, the Simon Wiesenthal Center, and the Stephen Roth Institute.

Who was Sir Ernest Henry Shackleton?

Irish-born Ernest Shackleton (1874–1922) was a renowned polar explorer and adventurer. He longed to be the first person to reach the South Pole. He made several attempts, but failed. His dream was realized in 1911 by two other men, Roald Amundsen and Robert Scott, on separate expeditions. Shackleton then proposed an expedition to cross the entire continent of Antarctica from the Weddell Sea to the Ross Sea on foot. His advertisement for crew for the journey read: "Men wanted for hazardous journey . . . bitter cold . . . small wages . . . safe return . . . doubtful." Five thousand men sought to join the expedition—26 were chosen. A stowaway also became a member of the crew after he was discovered. In 1914, as World War I was breaking out in Europe, Shackleton's ship, the *Endurance* (a name that would take on special meaning), set sail on this daring and dangerous expedition.

By January 1915, the *Endurance* was trapped, and eventually crushed, by treacherous ice floes in the Weddell Sea. Shackleton and his crew were stranded in Antarctica, facing savage cold and unforgiving conditions. They had no means of communication and limited equipment and supplies. Although the mission itself was a complete failure, it was equally successful and miraculous in the resourcefulness, heroism, and fortitude shown by this group of men under the command of Ernest Shackleton. All were rescued in 1916 and the legacy of their courageous tale of survival lives on.

Shackleton attempted another voyage to Antarctica in 1921, but died of a heart attack during the early part of the journey. The fame that eluded him in life found him in death. Shackleton's story survives and flourishes today through works based on the logs, diaries, and reflections of his voyages and the remarkable images recorded by Frank Hurley, the *Endurance*'s photographer.

To read more about Sir Ernest Henry Shackleton's 1914 expedition to Antarctica, see Caroline Alexander's book, *The Endurance*.

Why have so many famous people changed their names?

Authors, among others, may choose to use a pen name or a nom de plume. This is a pseudonym or a false name similar to the stage names or screen names adopted by some actors and other celebrities. Authors use an assumed name to conceal their identity or to create multiple identities for different types of work. A stage or screen name may be used by those who believe their own name to be difficult to pronounce or to remember, inappropriate for the image that they wish to project, or for other reasons. Some people legally change their name, while others keep their given name, but use a stage or pen name for professional purposes. Some well-known individuals who use (or used) names other than their birth names are listed below.

Real Name	Profession	Stage or Pen Name
David Robert Jones	singer/musician	David Bowie
Samuel L. Clemens	author	Mark Twain and Sieur Louis de Conte
Charles Lutwidge Dodgson	author	Lewis Carroll
Caryn Johnson	actress/comedienne	Whoopi Goldberg

What is WD-40?

WD-40 is a common household product used for many purposes, including lubricating squeaky doors, cleaning crayon marks off walls, and protecting against rust. It is a petroleum-based product named in 1953 by its inventor, Norm Larsen. Larsen was one of three chemists working on creating an industrial rust-preventing solvent for the Rocket Chemical Company of San Diego, California, to protect the outer skin of aerospace missiles from corrosion due to moisture buildup. The process to prevent corrosion involved the displacement of water. On his 40th attempt, Larsen succeeded. The name WD-40 stands for Larsen's Water Displacement, 40th attempt! In 1958 the product was packaged for sale for everyday use. The Rocket Chemical Company was renamed the WD-40 Company in 1969 and it still exists today.

For additional information on WD-40, visit www.wd40.com.

What is a Jake Brake?

Jake Brake is a registered trademark of Jacobs Vehicle Systems, a company that manufactures engine and exhaust brakes primarily for large trucks and RVs. Because of its trademark, the company rightfully asks the assistance of the public to notify it of the use of their product's name on signs and the like. Despite its trademark, however, the term has been somewhat generalized and is often used by individuals to identify all compression-release engine-braking systems, much like how the trademarked names of Band-Aid, Jell-O, and Q-tip are now used. Compression braking is a braking system that is typically installed on diesel big rigs to reduce the wear on the regular wheel brakes. They work to assist the driver in braking the truck, especially when negotiating long downhill grades. The brake involves using the truck's engine itself to supply braking power similar to downshifting a car. However, compression braking is more powerful and effective than down-

shifting because it turns the normally power-producing engine into a power-absorbing air compressor that creates drag. This action slows the truck down in proportion to the engine's revolutions per minute (rpm).

The noise that is emitted during compression braking is a distinctive roar that signals the release of air that has built up in the process. According to Jacobs Vehicle Systems, if the noise is excessive, it is the result of a truck with faulty, modified, or defective compression brakes. Although studies have shown that properly working engine brakes emit sound no louder than a powerful lawnmower, many communities have enacted ordinances against the use of compression brakes because the frequency of the sound tends to carry and is particularly noticeable.

For additional information about the Jake Brake, visit www.jakebrake.com.

What is the official name of London's Big Ben?

The official name of this famous London landmark is St. Stephen's Tower, which features the Great Clock of Westminster, but the tower and clock are usually called *Big Ben* by Londoners and people throughout the world. The 316-foot-tall clock tower forms part of the Houses of Parliament. Big Ben, however, is actually the name of the 13.5-ton hour bell that hangs within the tower, reportedly named after the first commissioner of works, Sir Benjamin Hall—a man of considerable size. Big Ben, 9 feet at its maximum diameter, is the largest of five bells in the tower and rings in the note of E.

The current Big Ben is a recasting of the original 16-ton bell that was cracked beyond repair in 1857 while being tested before installation in the clock tower. The bells of the Great Clock, with the smaller, second version of Big Ben, first rang out over the city in 1859. Two months later, Big Ben once again cracked, but was made functional by turning the bell and by the installation of a smaller bell hammer.

What is the origin of school as we know it today and who is responsible for the concept?

Public schooling in America took shape in the middle of the 19th century in the form of "common schools." Often called the father of the common school and of modern education, Horace Mann envisioned schools that were funded by local property taxes and governed by local committees with modest state legislation. He viewed schooling for all children as "the great equalizer," a forum for political stability and social harmony. Until this point in time, formal schooling was not considered essential for children and was typically available only to those whose families could afford it.

Schooling quickly became a vehicle to escape poverty and a symbol for achieving the American dream for everyone regardless of religion or station in life. Although curriculum and other aspects of education have changed dramatically over the years, receiving a formal education continues to be a desirable and coveted achievement among most Americans.

Who invented the game of basketball?

The game of basketball was created in 1891 by Dr. James Naismith, a Canadian-born educator, author, veteran, minister, and medical doctor. *Basket Ball*, as Naismith called the game, was developed at the International YMCA Training School (now Springfield College) in Springfield, Massachusetts, where he was employed as a physical education instructor. Naismith was asked by his superior to develop an interesting indoor game to help 18 rowdy male students better endure the long, harsh New England winter. The result was a game played with a soccer ball and two peach baskets nailed to a balcony 10 feet above the floor at each end of the gym. There were nine players per "team," playing the game with 13 basic rules. The school janitor used a ladder to retrieve the ball from the peach basket when a player scored. Women's basketball originated in 1892 when Senda Berenson Abbott, a gymnastics instructor, modified and adapted Naismith's rules for her students at Smith College in Northampton, Massachusetts.

In its early days, basketball was often a rather violent sport. Brawls among the players were common. A wire cage was built around some courts to protect the players from fans who threw things at the players or tried to burn them with cigarettes. Despite the violence, the game grew in popularity and debuted as a team sport in the 1936 Olympics in Berlin. Today it is estimated that basketball is played in more than 170 countries worldwide.

To learn more about the game of basketball, visit www .hoophall.com.

Why does the Tower of Pisa lean?

The Tower of Pisa is actually a bell tower of a cathedral in an area known as Piazza dei Miracoli in Pisa, Italy. It stands approximately 190 feet tall and has 293 steps. Construction began in 1173 and, after two long delays, was completed about two hundred years later. Although a beautiful structure, the Tower of Pisa owes its fame to the peculiarity of its leaning. Scholars, engineers, and builders generally agree that the leaning of the structure is the result of its being built on the unstable, soft silt of a buried riverbed. Seasonal fluctuations in the water table have also influenced the leaning of the tower. The addition of a walkway near the tower in the 19th century further disturbed the soil. Over the years, as the building of the tower progressed and for centuries afterward, various corrective architectural measures have been taken to offset the problem. All attempts failed and in 1990 the Italian ministry closed the structure to the public, fearing that the tower was in imminent danger of toppling over.

Efforts to stabilize the tower continued and engineers were able to "steer" the building into a more upright position by approximately 18 inches by removing soil around the tower at strategic locations. This stabilized the tower, but did not correct the problem to the point of visually affecting its famous tilt. The project cost approximately 53 billion lire ($25 million) and the tower was reopened to the public in December 2001.

To learn more about the Tower of Pisa, visit http://torre .duomo.pisa.it.

Who is Yogi Berra?

Yogi Berra, born on May 12, 1925, is a legend in the sport of baseball. He is best known as a catcher and clutch hitter for the New York Yankees. He also served as manager of the New York Yankees, player-coach for the New York Mets, and coach with the Houston Astros. He is a 15-time All-Star, three-time MVP, and winner of 10 world championships during his baseball career. He was elected to the National Baseball Hall of Fame in 1972. This World War II navy veteran, husband, father of three, and grandfather of 10 has resided in Montclair, New Jersey, for decades.

A humble and humorous man, Yogi Berra is also widely known for his quotable "Yogi-isms." Examples include:

- It ain't over til it's over.
- You can observe a lot by watching.

* When you come to a fork in the road, take it!
* The future ain't what it used to be.

To learn more about Yogi Berra, visit www.yogi-berra.com or www.baseballhalloffame.org.

What was the Trojan horse?

The Trojan War in Greek mythology was a war between the Greeks and the Trojans. As told by Homer in *The Odyssey*, the Greeks won the war by using a gigantic, wooden, hollow horse. Armed Greek soldiers hid inside the horse while the remainder of the Greek army pretended to retreat. The Trojans, thinking that they had beaten the Greeks and seeing the huge horse that the Greeks had left behind, decided to claim the horse as their own. That night while the Trojans were sleeping, the Greeks climbed out of the wooden horse and, joined by the rest of the Greek army, sacked Troy and burned it to the ground.

What is a nimrod?

A nimrod is a hunter. The term is taken from the name of Nimrod from the Old Testament. Nimrod is referred to, among other accomplishments, in Genesis 10:8–9 (New International Version) as "a mighty warrior on the earth" and "a mighty hunter before the Lord." Because of his repute as a great hunter, his name became synonymous with one who is devoted to or skilled at hunting.

Today the term *nimrod* is also used to identify someone who is silly, foolish, stupid, or boring. According to the *American Heritage Dictionary*, this usage likely came from the cartoon character Bugs Bunny's mocking of Elmer Fudd, a dithering, hapless hunter, as "poor little nimrod." Examples of using nimrod are:

> ❧ My lab partner is a total nimrod. She can't distinguish a beaker from a pipette.
> ❧ All he talks about is his computer. What a nimrod!

What is the Bermuda Triangle?

The Bermuda Triangle is a geographical area in the rough shape of a triangle as defined by the location of Bermuda, Puerto Rico, and Miami, Florida. The Bermuda Triangle is infamous for the seemingly high number of people, ships, and aircraft that have disappeared from the ocean and from the air in it. The area of the Bermuda Triangle is unofficial and is not designated or recognized by most geographical organizations. Recorded problems detected in this area, also called the Devil's Triangle, began with Christopher Columbus's reporting of compass irregularities, strange lights, and unidentified animals while in the region. Hysteria regarding the Bermuda Triangle was fueled in 1945 with the disappearance of five U.S. Navy Avenger torpedo bombers. Numerous books and cinematic ventures have chronicled the mystery and intrigue of events in the Bermuda Triangle.

Despite intense public interest and multiple notable unexplained incidents, the U.S. Coast Guard reports that incidents that occur in the Bermuda Triangle compare similarly to other highly trafficked maritime areas in the world. Accidents still occur, of course, but the advent of communication technology has all but eliminated "unexplained" or "without a trace" disappearances. Despite the temptation to believe in paranormal or other supernatural explanations, the probable explanation for occurrences in the Bermuda Triangle is the force of natural elements and/or human error.

What is a musketeer?

A musketeer is a soldier whose primary weapon is a musket. Musketeers became an important part of fighting forces in Europe and

certain Eastern countries. Musketeers are believed to have originated in 1622 in the French court of Louis XIII. Musketeers served
on foot and, sometimes, on horseback. They also served as an elite
cadre of bodyguards for the king when he traveled. Musketeers
proved to be effective soldiers and their popularity and utility
spread. Church officials and noblemen often trained private musketeers to protect and defend their interests including property, family
members, and associates. Due to the expense of maintaining com-
panies of musketeers, their use fell out of favor over the years.

The legend of musketeers was forever sealed in 1844 by Alexan-
dre Dumas in his novel, *The Three Musketeers* (*Les Trois Mousque-
taires*). Set in seventeenth-century France, the main character was
accompanied in his adventures by three friends (musketeers) who
were immortalized in literature by their familiar motto, "One for
all and all for one." Today, *musketeer* is often used as a term of
friendship and trust.

What is a puppy mill?

A puppy mill is a commercial dog breeding business where financial
considerations outweigh humane conditions for the animals involved. Typically, these operations are large scale, involve the
breeding of multiple breeds of dogs, and, according to their critics,
provide inadequate shelter, food, veterinary care, and/or socializa-
tion opportunities. Facilities are often overcrowded, unsanitary,
poorly ventilated, or inadequately protected from the elements.
Puppies from puppy mills are routinely sold to pet shops for resale
or are sold directly to consumers via the Internet or newspapers.
These operations are irresponsible and in many cases are operated
illegally and counter to laws designed to protect animals.

Responsible breeders care deeply for the health and well-being
of parent dogs and their puppies. They are also careful about the

people who purchase their puppies and frequently require that prospective buyers undergo some type of screening or interview process. When buying a purebred puppy, the American Kennel Club (AKC) recommends buying from a responsible and well-respected breeder. They advise that you ask to see at least one of the puppy's parents and that you pay attention to how the dogs interact with the breeder. See www.akc.org for additional information.

How did the flea market get its name?

The most probable origin of the name *flea market* comes from the French *le marché aux puces*, literally translated as "market with fleas." Named after certain open-air markets in Paris, many people, particularly those of unfortunate circumstances, would congregate to sell their secondhand goods. It was widely believed that these goods and wares harbored fleas—and in many cases they actually did! Additionally, because things associated with fleas are often deemed cheap, shabby, and/or unclean (i.e., flea bag hotel, flea-bitten dog), the description seemed particularly appropriate.

The first printed English use of *flea market* dates to the 1920s. Contemporary flea markets are popular places to buy and sell all sorts of items whose reputation has risen considerably higher than their humble beginnings.

What is a medicine ball?

A medicine ball is a heavy ball used in many gyms, rehabilitation centers, and training facilities. Typically weighing 8 to 12 pounds, it is sometimes called an exercise or fitness ball and is used for conditioning, strength training, general fitness exercise, and plyometrics (certain routines designed to improve explosive bursts or moves in athletics). Most medicine balls today are made of rubber with a textured surface for a better grip.

A medicine ball is approximately the size of a volleyball or basketball and therefore can be readily incorporated into group or individual exercise regardless of one's age or athletic ability. Although it serves many of the same purposes as using weights, it is safer to toss and more comfortable to rest on body areas than other types of heavy objects.

The medicine ball as we know it today originated in the late 1800s. It was not named *medicine ball* until World War I, when navy medics stuffed rags and kapok (mattress and life-preserver stuffing) in leather casings for seamen to toss to one another to help alleviate seasickness. However, seamen quickly found other purposes for medicine balls by using them in a variety of games to combat boredom while at sea.

What is the origin of the term *salary*?

Salary is a word used to describe wages or what one is paid for work rendered. In ancient Rome, salt was quite expensive and considered to be a valuable and highly marketable commodity. Soldiers and civil servants were paid a *salarium*—from the Latin *sal*, meaning salt. In other words, soldiers were paid their salaries in salt, or at least partially so. From this practice, we can also understand the origin and meaning of often-used phrases such as "worth your salt," "salting away," and "salt of the earth." Salt has even been traded with a value, ounce for ounce, rivaling gold. In fact, coins in China were at one time made of compressed salt.

Thanks to modern mining and desalinization techniques, salt is a compound that we now often take for granted because of its abundance and low cost. Historically, from antiquity through the 1800s, this was not the case. Because procuring salt was dependent on the location of salt deposits, access to brine, and/or the means or knowledge needed to produce salt, the "have-nots" were always at the mercy of the "haves" politically, socially, and economically—even to the point of inciting or altering the course of warfare.

If John Sr. passes away, does John Jr. take Sr. as part of his name?

The use of senior (Sr.) and junior (Jr.) for a surname suffix (also called an *extension*) is a relatively new Western custom used for a father and, usually, a first born son given the exact same name. As late as the 19th century, the terms senior and junior were used, but often as uncle-nephew or cousin-cousin namesakes—or even for unrelated males with the same name to differentiate the older one from the younger. The second (II) is correctly used as a social suffix when a son is named with the exact name of a grandfather, uncle, or cousin, for example.

There are neither firm rules of etiquette nor precedence of tradition governing suffix usage upon the death of a man. In other words, would Edward Coe Smith Jr. become Edward Coe Smith Sr.

upon the death of his father? This varies from family to family and is typically a matter of individual preference. "Moving up" a suffix is less frequently done as it tends to cause legal, financial, and social confusion. Doing this tends to negate the prospect of having future males named IV, V, VI, and so on—although there are notable examples where this is considered a desirable tradition, such as August A. Busch IV.

What is the difference between a first cousin and a second cousin?

Family relationships can be quite confusing. Your cousins are the children of an aunt or uncle. For example, if your mother's sister has a son, he is your cousin, your first cousin to be specific (typically referred to simply as a cousin). First cousins have the same biological grandparents as you do. If your mother's cousin has a son, he is your second cousin.

To further complicate matters, we occasionally hear the word *removed* associated with cousins. Your first cousin *once removed* may be either the child of your first cousin (actually a second cousin) or the child of your grandaunt or uncle (sister or brother of a grandparent). Being *removed* by definition indicates that the person is of a different generation than you. Once removed indicates a difference of one generation, twice removed a difference of two generations, and so on.

A good website to help sort out family relationships is www.genealogy.com.

How do they get all of that information into a computer?

Today's computers can store a great deal of information. Most people store software programs on their home computers that allow them to create (and save) documents, spreadsheets, presentations, and photos. There are many different kinds of software available and people choose what type of software they want. Some people, for example, like to play games on their computers, so they purchase and download game software onto their computers.

Today's computers also allow you to connect to the Internet. The Internet is a worldwide system of personal, business, government, and academic computer networks that allows computers to "talk" to each other. In order to be online (connected to the Internet), the user must have a modem attached to the computer or a direct digital link with an Internet service provider. Through the Internet, you can e-mail, chat, join discussion groups, instant message, and much, much more. You can also access the World Wide Web, which lets you find information on almost any topic under the sun. So, therefore, much of the information that you use on a computer isn't really *in* the computer; it is *accessed by* the computer.

What is topology?

Topology is a relatively new branch of mathematics that studies the properties of an object or thing. These properties do not change even if the object is distorted by stretching, compressing, or other forms of manipulation. Distortion is defined as the object *not* being torn, cut, or perforated in any way. If an object already has a hole, the hole is considered to be a property of the object and must remain in the transformed object. Topology is often referred to as "rubber sheet geometry." As a classic example, envision a doughnut made of clay. Through careful shaping and manipulation, the doughnut can be smoothly shaped into a mug, the handle of which is fashioned from the hole of the doughnut. Therefore, both objects, the doughnut and the mug, are considered to have the same topology. Another example is a subway or train map. These maps typically do not illustrate every twist or bend in the route but are simplified renditions of the actual route. A simplified map is topologically equal to an accurate map.

The father of the study of topology is Leonhard Euler (1707–1783). Euler, a Swiss mathematician, had remarkable powers of memory and reasoning. Euler's wonderings and observations led to the founding of the study of topology. Topology is often used for abstract or multidimensional studies in manufacturing, thermodynamics, and robotics.

What is *chisenbop*?

In mathematics, *chisenbop* is an ancient Korean method of finger counting. It dates back to the time when the abacus was used. Follow the steps below to see how to multiply by 9 using *chisenbop*:

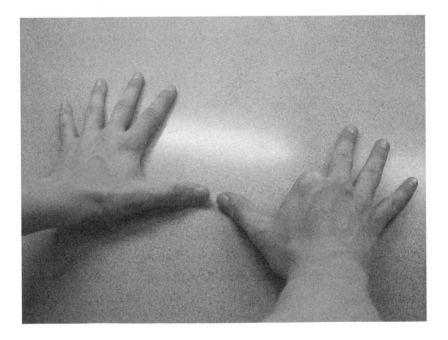

1) Extend all ten fingers in front of you, palms down.

2) Number them in your mind in numerical order, so that the pinkie to your far left is 1, the ring finger next to it is 2 and so on until the pinkie to the far right is 10.

3) Select a multiplication problem using the number 9. For example, 7×9.

4) Using your "numbered" fingers, lower your 7th finger (this should be the index finger on your right hand).

5) Look to see what fingers are still displayed: You should have 6 fingers showing to the left of your lowered index finger and 3 to the right of the lowered index finger.

6) Voila! $7 \times 9 = 63$.

Keep in mind that all mathematical functions are not this simple or even possible using *chisenbop*. This is simply one example of what can be done in this fashion.

What is a tessellation?

To appreciate tessellations, several factors must be understood. First, the word "tessellate" is defined as covering a plane or area with identical shapes or a combination of shapes that neither overlap nor leave gaps; theoretically, they could go on forever. Secondly, the shapes or "tiles" used must be regular polygons (one or more shapes) with each vertex being identical. The vertex is where corners of the tiles meet, forming 360°. Tessellations are most readily seen in ceramic tiling, brickwork, fabric design, or other practical arts. They are also seen in art, notably in works by M. C. Escher.

Tessellations can be one-dimensional or multidimensional in nature. Some tessellations break these "rules" by using modified shapes and/or not sharing common vertices or edges.

What does the Steelers emblem represent?

According to the official Pittsburgh Steelers website (www.steelers
.com), the now familiar Steelers emblem is based on the Steelmark
logo of the American Iron and Steel Institute (AISI) created by U.S.
Steel Corporation (now USX). It featured the word *Steel* and three
diamond shapes (called *hypocycloids*). Originally, for marketing
purposes, these hypocycloids represented steel's benefits: "steel
lightens your work, brightens your leisure, and widens your
world." During the 1960s, U.S. Steel returned the Steelmark program to the AISI and the logo came to represent the entire steel
industry. The hypocycloids came to correspond to the three materials used to make steel: yellow for coal, orange for ore, and blue for
scrap steel.

In 1962 at the suggestion of Cleveland's Republic Steel, the
Steelers decided to use the steel logo as their emblem and petitioned
the AISI to change the word *Steel* to *Steelers,* which was granted.
However, the Steelers were unsure if they liked their new logo, especially because it was not very visible on a gold helmet. Because of
this, the equipment manager was directed to temporarily place the
logo on one side of the helmet only. Experiencing their most successful season in franchise history that year, the Steelers decided to
change their helmet's color to black which, coincidentally, high-
lighted the new logo. And they decided to leave the logo on just one
side of the helmet. Even today, the Pittsburgh Steelers are the only
NFL team to display their logo on one side of their helmets only.

Why do we display yellow ribbons in times of war?

During the colonial Indian wars, the War of 1812, and the Civil
War, it was not uncommon for women to plait a ribbon of yellow

or regimental colors in their hair until their loved ones returned safely from war. Another root of this contemporary tradition may involve the yellow trim on Union soldiers' uniforms. Movies, particularly John Wayne's 1949 hit, *She Wore a Yellow Ribbon,* and the corresponding theme song of the same name, also referenced the wearing of yellow ribbons.

Displaying yellow ribbons as we know it today is a relatively new tradition sparked by another song, "Tie a Yellow Ribbon Round the Ole Oak Tree." Written in 1972 by Irwin Levine and L. Russell Brown, the lyrics were reportedly inspired by the legend of a Union soldier returning home from Andersonville Prison (Camp Sumter), a notorious Confederate prisoner of war camp. Levine and Brown updated and adapted this tale to tell the story of a young man hoping to reunite with his wife/girlfriend after a three-year prison term. The prisoner, nearing release, wrote asking her to tie a yellow ribbon on a particular oak tree if she still loved him. This was to serve as a signal as to whether or not she would have him back. He shared his story with the driver of the bus as he traveled toward her home. Fearing the worst, he closed his eyes. Amid the cheering of those on the bus, he opened his eyes to see the tree festooned with yellow ribbons! This song was popularized in 1973 when sung by Tony Orlando and Dawn. It was, however, Penelope Laingen, wife of hostage Bruce Laingen, the U.S. chargé d'affaires, who in 1979 tied a yellow ribbon around a tree at their home in Washington, D.C., in response to Iran's holding of her husband and 51 other American hostages. She vowed to display it until her husband returned home. Bruce Laingen was eventually released and when he got home, the yellow ribbon was still around the tree!

The use of yellow ribbons resurfaced in 1991 during Operation Desert Storm and at that point truly became a universally recognized American custom. Ribbons were commonly tied on homes, churches, businesses, and schools and were also worn on clothing. Since then, yellow ribbons continue to be widely used to express support of our troops and the wish for their safe return home. It is a symbol of safe homecoming, loyalty, encouragement, remembrance, and/or support for American troops and is not a statement one way or the other of one's opinion about war.

For more information about displaying yellow ribbons in times of war, visit www.loc.gov/folklife/ribbons/ribbons.html.

6

Cuisine

What is a Dutch oven?

A Dutch oven is a cooking pot typically characterized by thick walls and a tightly fitted, rimmed lid. For outdoor use, coals or embers can be heaped on the top as well as around the sides of this cookware, promoting even cooking much like that of a regular oven. Using a Dutch oven was popular with pioneers and homeowners of yesteryear. Early versions of Dutch ovens often had three legs to straddle live coals and a handle (bail) for carrying. They were made of cast iron.

Dutch ovens, quite similar to those used by pioneers, are also popular today for campers. Indoor versions, designed for stove top cooking, are often made of aluminum and have a flat, nonlegged bottom. Most contemporary Dutch ovens are manufactured by Lodge Manufacturing Company (www.lodgemfg.com). Lodge distinguishes the kitchen model as a "Dutch oven" and the legged, outdoor variety as a "camp oven." Either way, just about anything—breads, meats, vegetables, and desserts—can be cooked in a

Dutch oven. Foods prepared in Dutch ovens are renowned for their tenderness and tastiness!

The origin of the name "Dutch" oven is unclear. It is likely, however, that English settlers brought this type of cookware to America having imported it themselves from Holland.

What is the origin of the pretzel?

The origin of the pretzel is deeply rooted in legend. France, Italy, and Germany are each credited as its country of origin, but the exact place remains unknown. The most prevalent legend involves a young monk preparing unleavened bread for Lent. Christians of the day (circa AD 610) typically prayed by crossing their chests with their arms, each hand resting on the opposite shoulder. The monk, inspired by this prayer position, imitated this general shape with scraps of the leftover bread dough and gave the resulting "first pretzels" as a reward for children who said their prayers. The three holes are said to be representative of the Christian Holy Trinity. The monk called these treats *pretiola*, which is Latin for "little reward." Some sources claim that the word "pretzel" is from the German *bretzel*, and others claim it is from the Latin *brachium*, meaning "arm." In medieval times, pretzels were thought to bring good luck, prosperity, and spiritual wholeness to those who ate them.

Although some believe that pretzels were included with the provisions carried on the *Mayflower*, we know for sure that part of the history of the pretzel is tied to Pennsylvania. German immigrants (known as the Pennsylvania Dutch) brought what we call "soft pretzels" to America. The first commercial pretzels were baked by Julius Sturgis of Lititz, Pennsylvania. In 1861 Sturgis converted his traditional bread bakery into a pretzel-making business. The Sturgis Pretzel House is still in business today (www.sturgispretzel.com)!

The hard pretzel also had its origins in Pennsylvania (www.sny dersofhanover.com). One tale claims that a baker's apprentice fell asleep while baking traditional soft pretzels. The master baker, mistakenly thinking that the pretzels had not been baked long enough, rebaked them. The result was a tasty, crunchy treat—what we know as a "hard pretzel."

Today pretzels are one of America's favorite snack foods. They can be purchased (or made) soft or hard. They may be baked in many shapes, sizes, and flavors, salted or unsalted, and/or drizzled with chocolate or other confections. It is estimated the pretzel business in the United States alone tops $180 million per year.

How did Neapolitan ice cream get its name?

Neapolitan (nee-uh-*pahl*-uh-tuhn) ice cream is a block- or brick-shaped ice cream composed of multiple, usually three, distinct layers of flavors. Typically, the three flavors are chocolate, vanilla, and strawberry. This style of ice cream is often served in slices to better show the three layers and may be sold in boxes, tubs, or bars. The term *Neapolitan* can also refer to any molded or constructed dessert that has multiple layers.

The name itself is derived from Italy—specifically from the city of Naples. Residents of Naples are called Neapolitans and products from that area may be described as *Neapolitan*. In the 1800s, Naples became renowned for its spumoni (spuh-*moh*-nee or spoo-*moh*-nee), a three-flavored dessert usually comprised of cherry, chocolate, and pistachio ice cream. It was introduced to the United States late in that century, but its flavors were varied to appeal to popular American taste preferences and became what we call Neapolitan ice cream today.

What is London broil and is it of English origin?

London broil was originally a reference to flank steak or a recipe to prepare such a steak. Today, many boneless cuts of beef may be tagged in the supermarket as "London broil," which, of course, may vary in price. London broil is typically prepared by marinating the beef, then broiling it in the oven or cooking it on a grill.

Despite its decidedly British name, this dish is believed to be American in origin. It became popular after World War II when outdoor barbecuing became increasingly fashionable. A play on words based on a cockney (London) rhyme is believed to be a possible, yet ghastly, origin of the name *London broil*. A connection has been suggested between this rhyme, which refers to cannibalism, and the ill-fated Donner party (see What is the Donner Pass? in chapter 5).

What is a sous chef?

A sous (pronounced like the name "Sue") chef is one who is second in command in a restaurant or kitchen. The word *sous* is French for "under." The sous chef ranks below the head or executive chef and is considered the chef's principal assistant in the "brigade system." The brigade system was established by Georges-Auguste Escoffier, a renowned chef, teacher, and author of *Le Guide Culinaire*. Escoffier created this system to streamline and delegate employee tasks in large hotel kitchens. The responsibilities of the sous chef may include quality and portion control, visual appeal of the food, training other kitchen staff, sanitation issues, and cost factors. The sous chef is often the chef who plans and cooks the food, even if the head chef's name is on the menu!

Certification as a cook, sous chef, chef de cuisine, executive chef, master chef, and other positions in the kitchen is a process designed and managed by the American Culinary Federation, the nation's largest organization of cooks and pastry chefs. Points are awarded based on one's experience and education. Written and practical exams are also given. Once certified, a candidate has five years to work toward the next level of culinary proficiency.

Formal culinary education in America is only about 30 years old. Employers may or may not require certification when hiring chefs. Even though certification is desirable and a growing expectation, there is no substitute for good experience in a quality setting.

How did Thousand Island salad dressing get its name?

Thousand Island dressing, a variation of Russian dressing, is one of the most popular salad dressings in the United States. Although recipes vary, this sweet and chunky dressing is commonly made of mayonnaise or yogurt, ketchup, and a mixture of finely chopped hard-cooked eggs and vegetables (notably onion, pickle relish, peppers, and/or olives). The naming of this dressing can be traced to Clayton, New York. Renowned fishing guide George LaLonde assisted visiting fishermen in their quest for black bass and northern pike, plentiful in the waters of the Thousand Islands area of New York. Part of his hospitality included shore dinners prepared by his wife, Sophia.

May Irwin, a popular stage actress from New York City, and her husband hired George to guide their fishing vacation. The actress, also an avid cook and cookbook author, liked the salad dressing that Sophia served so much, she asked for and was given the recipe—dubbing it *Thousand Island dressing*. Ms. Irwin also shared Sophia LaLonde's recipe with fellow fisherman George C. Boldt, owner of the Waldorf-Astoria in New York City and other fine hotels. It was Boldt who is credited with spreading its fame.

How did oyster crackers get their name?

Oyster crackers are much like saltines, but are usually hexagonal (six sided) or round in shape and measure only about 15 millimeters in diameter. They are used most often as a topping on chowder or other soups. This practice dates back to ancient times as crackers, biscuits, and hardtack were easy to store and added bulk and nutrition when added to soups or stews.

Oyster crackers are not made with oysters. Today's oyster crackers evolved from the Trenton cracker, first made in 1848 by English immigrants Adam and John Exton in their Trenton, New Jersey, bakery. How they got the name *oyster crackers* remains a mystery, but it is speculated that because many chowders were made with oysters, an abundant and cheap food source years ago, these small crackers got their name by association. Another school of thought involves their shape. Most crackers of the day were pressed flat and were almost always square in shape. Oyster crackers, later baked by the National Biscuit Company, were puffy and more round or irregular in shape and, perhaps, diners thought they resembled oysters.

What is a chipotle?

Chipotle (chih-*poat*-lay) is a ripened jalapeño pepper that has been smoked or dried for use in cooking. They are hot, pungent, and quite flavorful. They are often described as having a sweet, smoky, chocolate-like taste. These peppers can be purchased dried, powdered, pickled, canned, or as a paste. Some say that whole, dried chipotles have the appearance of a cigar butt because they are tan or brown, 2 to 4 inches in length, and are wrinkled.

Chipotles were in known use for cooking in the Mexico City area in the time before the Aztec civilization. They are used in dishes throughout Mexico today and have become a wildly popular flavoring ingredient and appetizer in the United States and Canada. Chipotles are available at many grocery stores and fresh food markets. They are sometimes referred to as chipotle chilies and are used in sauces, salsas, soups, and in many other foods.

What is freezer burn?

The term *freezer burn* is an oxymoron (words in a phrase that seemingly have opposite meanings). After all, how could something *burn* in the freezer? The meaning of the phrase, however, is used to describe a specific phenomenon that occurs when food items are left in a freezer too long and/or are improperly wrapped. As the food is exposed to the low temperatures and dry air in the freezer, it becomes dehydrated (loses some of its water content), and dried, white or grayish brown patches appear. The food is still safe to eat when this occurs, but it is likely to be tough and tasteless. Many cooks simply trim away the affected areas and prepare the food as usual.

Food wrapping products, such as freezer bags and heavy duty aluminum or plastic wrap, are available to help prevent freezer burn. Plastic freezer containers and vacuum sealing are also options to help prevent this problem.

Ketchup or catsup—which is it?

This tomato-based condiment has been spelled many ways over time, including catsoup, katchup, catchup, even cornchop. The two prevailing spellings today are *ketchup* and *catsup*. Ketchup-maker H.J. Heinz Company used both spellings interchangeably until the beginning of the 20th century, when it began using *ketchup* exclusively because it resembled the word for a popular type of Chinese fish sauce, *ke-tsiap*. The recipe was altered dramatically, if not unrecognizably, to become what we know today as ketchup. Most major brands are now spelled *ketchup*, although one can still find the product labeled as *catsup*.

Ketchup, made primarily of tomato puree, vinegar, water, sugar, and spices, is the best-selling condiment in the Western world. Mustard runs a close second in popularity.

What is the origin of Buffalo wings?

Buffalo wings, or simply wings, are an American food favorite. They were first created in 1964 in Buffalo, New York, at the Anchor Bar, a restaurant owned by Frank and Teressa Belissimo. The most widely held version of how Buffalo wings were created involves the restaurant receiving an overshipment of chicken wings. Chicken wings, considered to be undesirable for the most part, were used primarily for soup stock or were often simply discarded. Mrs. Belissimo created a finger food using these wings with a hot sauce that she whipped up. Today Buffalo wings can be found in the simplest eatery to fast-food chains to fine dining establishments.

Recipes vary greatly and wings can be fried or baked, dredged in flour or not, and offered with different types of hot sauce. As with most food items, opinions vary as to how to make the "best" wings.

The original Belissimo recipe for Buffalo wings can be found in the cookbook *Totally Hot! The Ultimate Hot Pepper Cookbook*, or online at www.kitchenproject.com/history/AmericanHeritageRecipes/BuffaloWings.htm.

What is iodized salt?

Iodized salt is regular table salt to which minute amounts of iodine (potassium iodide or potassium iodate) have been added. In the early part of the 20th century, a condition known as goiter, an unsightly swelling of the neck, afflicted many Americans, especially those living in the Great Lakes area where iodine did not occur naturally in sufficient quantities. In other areas of the country, iodine is found in the soil and it is absorbed by plants (and the animals that eat the plants) which are then consumed by humans. Iodine is also found in seafood (and other food products).

Although the need for iodized salt is less than it was 100 years ago due to the active shipping of food items throughout the country, about 70% of all salt sold today for table and cooking use is iodized. Iodine is a necessary nutrient to maintain one's metabolism and other functions of the body. Since iodine was added to table salt in 1924, goiter has all but disappeared in America. Bigger problems than goiter, however, are also associated with a lack of iodine. Called Iodine Deficiency Disorder (IDD), conditions such as mental impairment, coordination problems, dwarfism, and other abnormalities may be manifested in those who ingest too little iodine. Although IDD is now quite rare in the United States, it remains a major health problem in other parts of the world.

Do mushrooms have any nutritional value?

The mushroom is actually a fungus. Those who love to eat mushrooms will likely describe their earthy taste or meaty texture. The mushroom comes in many varieties and can be used in many ways, including as an entrée, side dish, or snack. They can be served in the same ways that one would prepare many vegetables—fried, grilled, microwaved, sautéed, or raw. Mushrooms are very nutritious, too. Although the amounts may vary between mushroom types, mushrooms are good sources of protein, fiber, vitamins B_1, B_2, B_3, C, and D, niacin, potassium, phosphorus, iron, and other nutrients. They are low in, or free of, sodium, fat, and cholesterol. A few of the more popular mushroom varieties commercially available include shiitake, cremini, button, oyster, enoki, portobello, beech, and maitake mushrooms. (A note of caution: Some mushrooms are poisonous. When gathering mushrooms in the wild, be sure to know what you are doing and seek help in identifying all mushrooms before eating them.)

Pennsylvania is the number one state in the United States for mushroom production. Kennett Square, Pennsylvania, calls itself the "Mushroom Capital of the World" and is home to the Phillips Mushroom Museum. Visit www.phillipsmushroomfarms.com/farm.html for an excellent source of mushroom nutritional facts and other information about mushrooms in general.

What is the difference between black olives and green olives?

Actually, both green and black olives are the same fruit and they come from the same tree. There are over 50 varieties of the common olive, *Olea europaea*. Green olives are unripe when picked and, due to their extreme bitterness at this point, must be cured, then stored in brine, to make them edible. There are many "recipes" used to pickle the green olive for eating. These may vary from country to country and region to region.

In contrast, black olives are olives that remain on the tree until ripe. They become dark purplish brown to black in color. They are softer in texture and are considerably more mellow in taste. Olives are available for purchase in many forms—pitted, nonpitted, stuffed, and marinated, to name a few. They are popular as a cooking or salad ingredient, garnish, or simply by themselves. Olive oil is, of course, a product made from olives and requires a special process to produce.

Olives have been cultivated in the Mediterranean region for thousands of years. The olive tree is referred to in many classical works and in the Bible. The olive tree has a particularly impressive life span of 300 to 400 years and has long been a symbol of peace, happiness, and purity. Spain is the world's leading exporter of olives, although olives are also commercially grown in Italy, France, Australia, South Africa, and America (primarily in California).

What is a wok?

A wok (rhymes with clock) is a Chinese cooking pan with a convex bottom ranging in width from 1 foot to 4 feet in diameter. Widely, if not universally, used in Southeast Asia and China, the wok provides a range of cooking temperatures within the pan and is essential for stir-frying, steaming, stewing, braising, and deep-frying. Contemporary woks are made rounded or flat bottomed, one- or two-handled, and may or may not have a nonstick surface. Electric versions are also available. Flat-bottomed, nonstick, and electric woks are more common in Western countries. Steel is the preferred material for woks as it has the desired heat transfer properties.

It is believed that the wok originated in China, adapted from the invading Mongolian warriors who used their metal helmets and shields to cook their food. This provided a method of quick cooking that was also very fuel efficient. This is true of contemporary woks as well as they continue to exhibit these same qualities.

How did the macadamia nut get its name?

The macadamia (mack-uh-*day*-me-uh) tree is native to Australia. It is a subtropical evergreen. Growing about 30 to 40 feet high and almost as wide, the macadamia resembles a holly tree.

The tree was named by a botanist in honor of his friend, the Scottish-born chemist Dr. John McAdam, a noted lecturer in practical and theoretical chemistry at the University of Melbourne and a member of Parliament. Macadamia came from the surname McAdam!

Early settlers in Australia considered the tree to be simply ornamental. In time, they discovered the value of the delicious and nutritious nut that the tree produced. Exported to Hawaii at the end of the 19th century, the macadamia thrived in the year-round warm, moist climate and benefited from improved grafting techniques. In the 1920s growers learned how to more easily remove the hard shell from the nut. This was instrumental in spurring the commercial success of macadamias. Today Hawaii is the largest grower and exporter of macadamia nuts.

Is scrod a fish?

There is no specific fish called *scrod* (skrahd). When you see "scrod" on a menu or at the market, it is referring to a young fish, usually a cod, haddock, or pollock weighing 2.5 pounds or less when caught. It is suspected that the term came from the obsolete Dutch word *schrood*, meaning to slice or shred, as scrod is typically served split and boned. The use of the term *scrod* was first noted in 1841. Scrod is a lean, moderately firm, white meat with a mild flavor and is low in fat and calories. Scrod can be prepared by broiling, poaching, frying, baking, braising, and other methods. Scrod is often offered as the "catch of the day."

What is cinnamon?

Cinnamon is a spice commonly used today in cakes, cookies, beverages, and fruit recipes. Elsewhere, in the Middle East for example, it is used to flavor certain meat dishes. According to McCormick's *Spice Encyclopedia*, most of the cinnamon used in the United States comes from the *Cinnamomum burmannii* bush or tree and is imported from Indonesia. The yellow inner bark is stripped from the branches and dried. During the drying process, the bark curls into reddish brown quills or cinnamon sticks. The sticks can be used for various purposes or ground into a sweet yet pungent powder. *Cinnamomum zeylanicum*, grown in Sri Lanka (formally Ceylon), is considered to be the "true" cinnamon. However, due to its unique flavor, it is not widely used in America. Cinnamon and cinnamon-like spice is also produced in other parts of the world.

Cinnamon, considered a luxury item throughout most of its history, was typically used by the wealthy. The desire to acquire it played a role in the expansion of European colonies and the founding of the New World. Cinnamon has been prized for other uses throughout history as well. Ancient Egyptians used it as an embalming agent. Other cultures have used it in religious ceremonies, in burial rituals, as incense, in perfume, as medicine due to its antibacterial properties, and, in the days before refrigeration, to cover the taste of spoiling meats. Some of these uses are still employed today.

Is the tomato a fruit or a vegetable?

Botanically speaking, the tomato is a fruit. A fruit is the fleshy, edible part of the plant that contains the seeds. By this definition, squash, cucumber, watermelon, and green pepper are also examples of fruits. However, horticulturally speaking, the tomato is a vegetable as it applies to certain plants that are grown for an edible part, typically intended to be consumed during the principal part of a meal. As you can see, a case can be built to support your own point of view as to whether the tomato is a fruit or a vegetable!

Interestingly, even the tomato has had its day in court. In 1887 the United States Supreme Court ruled that the tomato is a vegetable. This suit was brought by a consortium of American growers against an American importer who was importing tomatoes, widely considered to be a fruit due to the botanical definition. Fruits were not subject to import taxes; vegetables were taxed. By ruling the tomato to be a vegetable, the importer had to pay the tariff, thus helping to protect crop development and the price of domestically grown tomatoes.

The tomato (*Lycopersicon lycopersicum*) is native to the Americas. Explorers took tomato seeds from the Aztecs and Incas back to

Europe. The French dubbed the tomato "the apple of love." The Germans called it "the apple of paradise." The English, however, believed that the tomato was poisonous. This concern carried over to the English colonists, but faded in part due to the popularity of tomato-based Creole cooking. Today tomatoes are considered to be a healthy source of vitamin A, vitamin C, and lycopene, an antioxidant. Florida and California are the top two tomato-producing states.

What makes popcorn pop?

Heat and pressure make popcorn "pop." Each kernel of popcorn (*Zea mays everta*) has a starchy center that contains moisture, ideally about 13.5%, and an extra hard exterior shell. Heat from the stove, microwave, or popper causes the moisture to turn into steam

and build up pressure within the kernel. When the pressure is high enough, the kernel explodes, essentially turning itself inside out! The white part of popcorn is the starchy center part of the popcorn kernel. If you look carefully at a piece of popcorn, you can still see the hard outer shell of the kernel. The shell's color can be off-white, golden, red, black, or other shades.

Popcorn was an important part of Incan, Aztec, and Native American culture. It was used for food, in headdresses, in necklaces, and for ceremonial purposes. Native Americans reportedly brought popcorn to the first Thanksgiving. At that time, a common method of making popcorn included heating an oiled ear of popcorn on a stick over a fire until the kernels popped. The popped kernels were then chewed off of the cob. Colonists often enjoyed popcorn as a breakfast cereal, served with milk or cream.

It is estimated that the average American consumes from 58 to 70 quarts of popcorn per year. Most of the world's popcorn is grown in Nebraska and Indiana.

Is a vegan a vegetarian?

A vegan (*vee*-gun) is a person who chooses not to consume or use animal products. Veganism is a form of vegetarianism as meat, poultry, and fish are avoided, but it also involves not consuming any animal by-products (such as honey, eggs, and dairy products) or using any animal products (such as fur, leather, wool, silk, and down). Other specific forms of vegetarianism are:

- *Ovo vegetarian:* One who does not eat meat, poultry, fish, or dairy products—but does eat eggs and egg products.
- *Lacto vegetarian:* One who does not eat meat, poultry, fish, or egg products—but does eat dairy products.
- *Lacto-ovo vegetarian:* One who does not eat meat, poultry, or fish—but does eat egg and dairy products.

Individuals become vegetarians for health, nutritional, religious, ethical, and/or other reasons. They may also vary in their degree of strictness in the observance of their diet and use of animal products. It is estimated that there are as many of 4.8 million adult vegetarians in the United States.

What is white chocolate?

White chocolate is not really chocolate at all. It is an ivory colored confection made with cocoa butter, but with no chocolate liquor. Chocolate liquor, which contains no alcohol, is the thick, dark paste that remains when the cocoa bean is processed and ground to remove the shell and cocoa butter. The presence of chocolate liquor is required by the U.S. Food and Drug Administration (FDA) in order for a product to legitimately be called *chocolate*.

Because there is no universally recognized standard to regulate white chocolate as yet, some white chocolate is made with vegetable fat rather than cocoa butter. White chocolate made with vegetable fat is considered inferior in taste and texture to that made with cocoa butter. Quality white chocolate is typically made of a mixture of sugar, cocoa butter, milk solids, lecithin, and vanilla.

Cocoa butter has very little chocolate flavor, but it contributes to chocolate's ability to remain solid at room temperature and provides a smooth characteristic in foods that contain it, as well as to other products such as soap, suntan lotions, and cosmetics.

What is a sardine?

There is actually no such fish as a sardine. What we call sardines are actually small or immature fishes in the herring family (*Clupe-*

idae). What are called sardines in northern European countries may be sild or brisling (types of herring). Likewise, in the northeastern United States, sardines may be other types of small herring. In France or Portugal, sardines are likely to be pilchards. In addition, it is not uncommon for any host of small, oily, silvery, edible fishes (nonherring) to be referred to as sardines. Sardines travel in large schools along coastlines throughout the world. They got their name from the canning process that was first developed in Sardinia (an island near Italy).

Sardines are typically packed in oil or water. If served fresh, they may be prepared grilled, broiled, fried, salted, smoked, or served in a variety of sauces. They are a good source of protein and are low in saturated fat. They are also high in omega-3 fatty acids, which are considered to be heart healthy. Sardine oil is used primarily as a lubricant and in some soap products.

Interestingly, the word *sardine* is regularly used to indicate a condition of being packed into something (as sardines are in a can). For example:

» We felt like sardines on the train.
» At the sleepover, all of my friends were sardined on the floor because we had but one bed.

On a menu, what does A.Q. mean?

Menus often feature confusing terms. A.Q. means "as quoted." This may also be noted on a menu as "market price." *A.Q.* and *market price* are typically associated with more expensive foods, such as certain types of seafood, where the price may vary seasonally.

Other terms seen on menus include:

Menu Term	Explanation
à la carte	A menu item that is priced separately and may be ordered individually as it suits the diner.
prix fixe	A complete, set meal of several courses offered for a fixed price.
table d'hôte	A complete meal of several courses where the diner chooses each course from those offered. The price of the main dish (the entrée) usually determines the price of the entire meal.

What is a pitted ham?

In culinary terms, *pitted* usually means the hard, nonedible part of a food has been removed. Examples of food that can be pitted include the cherry, olive, plum, nectarine, and peach, all of which have seeds or pits. The same principle applies to ham—that is, a whole, boneless ham may be referred to as a pitted ham. The term *pitted ham* is used more frequently in the Deep South.

There is also such a thing as a *pitted ham knife*. This type of knife is typically used to carve or debone larger cooked and/or cured meats that can crack and fall apart easily. The thinner, narrower blade presumably reduces contact with the meat, helping to keep the meat intact.

What is a maître d'?

A maître d' (may-tra-*dee*) is the shortened version of the French *maître d'hôtel*, translated as *master of the hall or hotel*. This is the job title given to a person who is in charge of taking reservations, seating people in a restaurant, and/or assigning waitstaff to various areas of the restaurant. Maître d's are typically associated with fine dining establishments of appreciable expense. They wield considerable power in restaurants that attract celebrities because having just the right table or being able to dine without reservations is a valued commodity. For an appropriate remuneration or simply the pride of being of service to certain patrons, maître d's can make things happen in a restaurant.

This position is also sometimes called headwaiter or captain; in less elite restaurants, the title of host, hostess, or manager may be used.

Why are some pistachios red?

The tradition of red pistachios comes to us indirectly from the Middle East. Due to the use of antiquated harvesting and processing methods in that part of the world, the occurrence of blemishes on pistachio hulls was quite common. Importers in other countries often used a red colorant to camouflage this damage in order to make the nuts more appealing to consumers. Additionally, in the 1930s, nuts and candies were often sold in vending machines. Red coloration made pistachios stand out, which resulted in higher sales. Red pistachios became the norm of the day.

Today, most pistachios are sold in their natural, tan state. According to the California Pistachio Commission (www.pistachios .org), domestic pistachios came on the market in the late 1970s. California pistachios, typically bigger than their imported counterparts, had clean, smooth shells with far fewer imperfections. These nuts grew in popularity among pistachio lovers, especially in concert with a growing American preference for natural qualities in foods. However, to some people, a pistachio is just not a pistachio unless it is red. Therefore, some U.S. pistachios are still dyed red to appeal to those who prefer them that way.

Who invented the tea bag?

The Chinese emperor Shen Nung is said to have accidentally created the drink of tea in 2737 BC when leaves from a nearby tea bush blew into a pot of water that he was boiling. Imported to Holland in 1610 by the Dutch India Company, tea grew in popularity in Europe, then America. Although coffee consumption outweighs that of tea in the United States today, tea is still widely enjoyed throughout the country.

Two variations in the preparation of tea occurred in America. The Englishman Richard Blechynden, distressed by the oppressive heat and sagging sales of hot tea at his pavilion at the 1904 World's Fair in St. Louis, Missouri, added ice to his tea; the new taste sensation, iced tea, was a success then—and now!

Second, the tea bag was invented, also inadvertently, by Thomas Sullivan in 1908 as a way to economize. To avoid the high cost of the traditional tin box used to store and transport loose tea, he placed tea samples in hand-sewn silk bags. Much to his surprise, rather than opening the bags and preparing tea in the customary fashion of using loose tea, his customers poured boiling water directly onto the bags or dropped them into boiling water. The idea caught on with gauze, then paper, largely replacing the silk bags.

How did corned beef get its name?

Corning is a form of curing meat and is unrelated to the vegetable we call "corn." In the days before refrigeration, meat was often preserved by dry curing, which involved packing it in "corns" (corn kernel–sized pellets) of salt. According to the U.S. Department of Agriculture (www.usda.gov), corning beef (hence, *corned* beef) originated in rural Ireland back before the days of refrigeration and was considered a traditional entrée for the Easter Sunday meal—usually a welcome dish after a meatless Lenten season.

Despite improved methods of preserving meat over time, the taste of corned beef remained popular in many countries and cultures, although today it is usually prepared by brining the beef in saltwater containing a variety of spices and flavorings such as peppercorns, bay leaves, garlic, and/or other regional favorites. Corned beef is often made with less tender portions of beef—round or brisket, for example.

Corned beef and cabbage is especially popular on St. Patrick's Day with Irish Americans who consider it a reminder of their Irish heritage. Reuben sandwiches and corned beef hash are other favorite corned beef meals.

What is buttermilk?

Originally, buttermilk was simply the liquid that remained after milk was churned into butter. Today, commercially available buttermilk is the product of "culturing" nonfat milk with certain microorganisms. This results in a fermented, off-white, tangy (acidic) milk greatly beloved for baking and drinking. When buttermilk is not readily available, cooks often add lemon juice or vinegar to regular milk to simulate buttermilk in a recipe.

7

Geography and Community

What is a cartographer?

A cartographer (kar-*tog*-ra-fer) is a person who makes maps. Cartography involves the actual drawing of a map or can refer to the use of maps for research, travel, or scientific information. Also, the study of maps for historical, artistic, or scholarly purposes is considered to be a form of cartography.

Maps have been needed and studied by man from prehistoric times to the present. Research suggests that mapmaking developed in various regions of the world simultaneously and has taken many forms, including cave drawings, writings on papyrus scrolls, and today's computer-generated maps. The computer has provided the technology that has replaced, in large measure, traditional drafting techniques. Satellite imagery has also greatly enhanced the cartographer's ability to create accurate maps.

The art and science of making maps is ever changing. Cartography, for many, is a fascinating hobby and is still an excellent career choice.

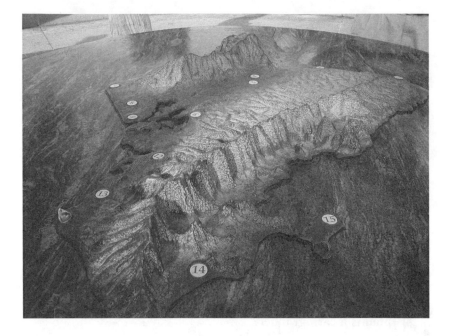

Why is Pennsylvania called the Keystone State?

The word *keystone* is an architectural term referring to a central, wedge-shaped stone in an archway. The keystone holds the other stones in the arch in place. This concept is clearly applicable in several instances regarding Pennsylvania. Geographically and strategically, Pennsylvania is a bridge of sorts that connects the northeastern states and the southeastern states. Visually, it was central on the U.S. map when the Constitution was created. Politically, Pennsylvania held an authoritative role in the economic, social, and legislative development of the new nation.

No one in particular is credited with coining the term *Keystone State*, but it was in use in the early 1800s, as evidenced by Pennsylvania being toasted as "the keystone in the democratic arch" at a Thomas Jefferson Republican rally.

What is a Hoosier?

A Hoosier (with a capital *H*) is someone who is a native or resident of Indiana. It is an appellation used primarily, although certainly not exclusively, in the southern part of the state and is paralleled in usage to North Carolinians being called Tarheels, Oklahomans being called Sooners, or Ohioans being called Buckeyes. Students and alumni of Indiana University are also nicknamed *Hoosiers*. The origin of the term *hoosier* is uncertain. According to the Indiana University Alumni Association (www.indiana.edu/~alumni/fun/hoosier.html) and other sources, there are various theories which include:

- In 1825 contractor Samuel Hoosier (or Hoosher) was building a canal on the Ohio River. His workers, many of whom hailed from Indiana, came to be called Hoosier's men or Hoosiers.
- Early settlers possibly called out "who's here?" to determine if the person at their door was a friend or foe. (Or worse, "whose ear?" to identify the body part after a particularly vicious fight.)
- Hoosier may be a derivative of the Cumberland (English) dialect of "hoozer," meaning "high hills."

It is clear, however, that in the early days of using the term many associated it with those who were poor, poorly educated, uncouth, rough, and/or lawless. Some contemporary dictionaries still define *hoosier* along these lines for one of their listed definitions. Popularized by Edward Eggleston's *The Hoosier School-Master* in the 1800s, and in John Finley's poem, *The Hoosier's Nest*, Indianans began to use the term as a point of pride associating the nickname with traditional, conservative, homespun values in keeping with their reputation for honesty and a strong work ethic.

What is the Coudersport Ice Mine?

One of Pennsylvania's natural wonders certainly includes a peculiar natural phenomenon called the Coudersport Ice Mine. Located in Potter County, about 4 miles east of Coudersport, the ice mine has provided fascination and folklore for over 100 years. Legend has it that the local Native Americans in the late 19th century had a great deal of pure silver ore. The settlers in the region, naturally, wanted to find the location of their silver mine. Using a rod typically used to locate water or minerals, ice was found instead, along with human bones and fossilized plant and animal artifacts. Silver was never located. Once a tourist attraction, the ice mine is now closed to the public, at least for the time being.

What makes the Coudersport Ice Mine unique is the occurrence of ice in the *summer* and little or none in the *winter*! *Ice mine* is actually a misnomer, for the mine itself is more like a pit or vertical shaft that measures approximately 40 feet deep and 8 feet wide. During the late spring and summer (ice season), large, crystal clear icicles, frozen slabs of ice, and/or other icy formations appear. Scientists call this phenomenon a *coldness trap* or *glacière*. The colder winter air is heavier, so it falls to the bottom of the cave. The cracks and crevasses of the pit freeze, preventing much water from entering. Even though the air in summer is warmer, the colder air cannot escape and is trapped there. The shaft is almost always cold enough to freeze water. However, with warmer weather comes the melting snow and ice of winter, which refreezes upon arrival when it seeps into the pit. By the end of the autumn months, the temperature in the pit increases enough to thaw the formations—and the cycle is repeated.

Which city in America is called the Pittsburgh of the South?

Birmingham, Alabama, has this nickname. Birmingham, located in the northern portion of the state, is Alabama's largest city. The city was named after Birmingham, England, due to that city's iron and coal industry. Birmingham grew as a city near significant deposits of iron, coal, limestone, and dolomite and experienced tremendous growth in the early 1900s due to steel and iron production. Because of the industrial parallels with Pittsburgh, Pennsylvania, the nickname stuck and was in popular use for decades. The nickname "Magic City" was also used due to the amazingly rapid growth of the city.

A 56-foot statue of Vulcan, the mythical god of forge and fire, was built in Birmingham to showcase the booming steel industry at the turn of the century. The statue is believed to be the largest cast-metal statue in the world and was built for the 1904 St. Louis World's Fair. After falling into a state of disrepair over the years, Vulcan is now restored to its original condition. Much like Pittsburgh, however, the steel industry in Birmingham waned and diversification was necessary. Today Birmingham manufactures metal products, machinery, and other industrial goods from raw materials brought in from other places, but it is more known for biotechnical pursuits, finance, and for being home to many corporate headquarters. Still shadowed in some ways by the racial turmoil and violence that occurred there in the 1960s, Birmingham is a vital city very proud of its steel heritage and promising future.

What is a Buckeye?

The term *buckeye* is widely used in Ohio, far beyond Ohio State University's team name. Residents are nicknamed *Buckeyes*. Furthermore, in 1953, the Ohio buckeye tree (*Aesculus glabra*) officially became the state tree of Ohio, and the official nickname, the "Buckeye State," was established. The state flag of Ohio features a white circle with a red center. This represents the buckeye nut as well as the O for Ohio. Buckeye nuts, mildly toxic if eaten, are often carried by individuals as a good luck charm. According to the Ohio State University website (www.osu.edu), the buckeye tree, abundant in the Ohio Valley, is native to Ohio and was unfamiliar to settlers arriving from the East. A beautiful tree featuring five-fingered leaflets, the buckeye has little practical value, but it is a tough tree—difficult to destroy or uproot, grows where others won't, and very adaptable—hence the appeal of the nickname comparison.

In Hawaii, what does *aloha* mean?

Aloha is commonly known as a word of friendly greeting or farewell. However, it means much more than this. In Hawaii, and among those who understand the complexity and multiple levels of this word, it can also indicate unconditional forms of affection, mutual regard, love, empathy, compassion, hospitality, and the like. This attitude or philosophy is not easily translated into English and it is referred to as the *Aloha Spirit*, which is more a state of mind or aura of being that signifies the respectful treatment of people or a

deep understanding and appreciation of the human spirit. In fact, the *Aloha Spirit* is written into state law in Hawaii (section 5–7.5) and includes language that addresses qualities of kindness, unity, agreeableness, humility, and patience.

Aloha is literally translated as "the breath of life." Native Hawaiians consider this to emanate from within a person's heart, mind, and actions. It is characterized by knowledge and wisdom—a form of inner peace. It is said to have originated by the native Hawaiians and given as a gift to all the people of Hawaii.

For details on the *Aloha Spirit*, visit www.geocities.com/~olelo/ alohaspirit.html.

Do homing pigeons "home" by way of geographical features?

Homing pigeons are a variety of the domesticated rock pigeon (*Columba livia*). They are characterized by their extraordinary ability to find their way back to their own nest from hundreds of miles away. Research suggests that several factors are involved in homing pigeons being able to *home*. It is believed that these birds navigate by earth's magnetic field and by astronomical (position of the sun and stars) means, especially when flying in unfamiliar territory. When a route is more familiar, they are known to use natural and man-made landmarks, even to the point of following roadways. Their sense of smell may also contribute to their homing abilities. Homing pigeons average about 30 miles per hour when flying short or moderate distances, but can accelerate up to 60-mile-per-hour bursts on occasion.

Homing pigeons, also called homers or messenger pigeons, have played an important role in world history since antiquity. Relatively recent uses are exemplified by their postal functions in relaying news and stock market information in Europe in the mid-1800s and as true "air mail" from 1898 to 1908 between New Zealand and Australia. These birds also served a critical role in World War I and

World War II as couriers of vital messages. They are credited with contributing to battle victories and the saving of many lives in wartime. Several of these birds were actually decorated for meritorious service to the war effort.

The usefulness of military homing pigeons has waned due to advances in communication technologies and most pigeon corps have been discontinued; however, the Austrian army recently reinstated a carrier pigeon corps as a backup to its computer systems, and pigeons were used by the U.S. Marine Corps in 2003 in Kuwait as chemical warfare detectors (much like canaries in coal mines). Today, homers are primarily enjoyed by hobbyists, pigeon racing enthusiasts, and as show birds.

Why are Oklahomans called Sooners?

The nickname *Sooners* originated in Oklahoma at the time of the land run of 1889. Indian lands in the Oklahoma Territory were considered to be "unappropriated" and therefore available for distribution to interested settlers. Rules specified when settlers could cross boundary lines and lay claim to land for a homestead and a new life. However, opportunists sneaked into the Oklahoma Territory prior to the legal time and, therefore, had an unfair advantage over the thousands who lined up on the border at the designated time to make their run. Because these poachers entered the territory *too soon*, they were called *Sooners*. Many disputes and legal wrangles ensued—a pattern repeated when subsequent lands were opened for settlement, too.

Naturally, the name *Sooner* was originally used disparagingly as these people were considered to be outright thieves. However, when the University of Oklahoma chose the nickname *Sooners* for its football team in 1908, opinion began to soften to the point where

now Oklahoma is nicknamed the *Sooner State* and its residents, *Sooners*—a point of pride symbolic of progressivism, ingenuity, and ambition.

Why is Pennsylvania called a commonwealth?

Calling Pennsylvania a "commonwealth" dates back to June 18–25, 1776, with the writing of Pennsylvania's first constitution. This constitution used both "state" and "commonwealth" in its wording. Both terms were also used in the constitutions of 1790, 1838, 1874, and 1968. Carpenter's Hall in Philadelphia is considered to be the "official" birthplace of the Commonwealth of Pennsylvania, affirmed in Harrisburg in 1982 by House Resolution 180. Although the State Seal of Pennsylvania features the term "state," "commonwealth" is considered a traditional and official title and is used for legal business conducted by the state. The terms "state" and "commonwealth" are correctly used today interchangeably.

The origin of the word is English, meaning common "weal" or the well-being of the citizenry. "Commonwealth" is also the designation of three other states—Virginia, Massachusetts, and Kentucky.

What is a benchmark in topographic mapping?

The United States Geographical Survey (USGS) is charged with the responsibility for charting and producing maps of all kinds. One type of map is a topographic map, which depicts terrain by showing ground elevation including natural and man-made features. These maps are typically a two-dimensional representation of horizontal and vertical positions of terrain using contour lines, coloration, and various symbols. Topographic maps are valuable tools for cartographers, surveyors, engineers, governmental agencies, industries, and naturalists.

The USGS was established in 1879 and produced its first topographic map during that year. During the earlier days of mapping the United States, this process was extremely expensive, labor-intensive, and dangerous. In accordance with the National Map Accuracy Standards, originally issued in 1941, precision in mapmaking is required so that maps are consistent in appearance and detail. As part of assuring this, brass markers called *benchmarks* were installed by the USGS at survey stations to establish control points.

Topographic mapping today is generally accomplished via aerial photography and satellite imagery. Still a laborious process in its own way, computer technology has improved map standardization and reduced the necessity for exhaustive fieldwork.

Visit the USGS website at www.usgs.gov for a wealth of interesting and educational information about maps and mapping.

Why is the motto of New Hampshire "Live Free or Die"?

The origin of New Hampshire's motto, Live Free or Die, came from General John Stark, a distinguished hero of the Revolutionary War. The phrase was taken from the text of a toast that General Stark penned in 1809. The general was unable to attend the 32nd anniversary reunion of the 1777 Battle of Bennington (Vermont) due to poor health, but contributed by sending a toast which read, "Live Free or Die; Death Is Not the Worst of Evils." It was not until 1945 when World War II was coming to a victorious end, however, that the words "Live Free or Die" were made the official state motto of New Hampshire.

The state motto is not without controversy, however. There is currently a move afoot to change it to "You're going to love it here." Supporters of this change claim that the current motto is unwelcoming and simply too belligerent. Proponents of keeping the motto argue that the aforementioned is a commercial slogan, not a motto. They assert that the motto as it currently reads is an important part of New Hampshire's history and culture—and the debate rages on.

What are the dominant religions of the United States?

Christianity is by far the largest religion in America, with 87% of the country identifying themselves as Christian. Of this majority, 58% is Protestant, 27% is Roman Catholic, 1% is Mormon, and 1% is Eastern Orthodox.

Three percent of the population is Jewish, while another 3% belong to various lesser populated or practiced denominations, religions, sects, or orders. The remainder of the population embraces no specific religious preference.

Keep in mind, these percentages are approximate and shift and change depending on the source consulted and the year surveyed. Interestingly, many religions are not specifically mentioned as part of the Gallup Poll or other surveys. Muslims, for example, are thought to comprise less than 3% of the population in the United States, but, again, specific numbers are difficult to determine.

Who becomes president if something happens to the president of the United States?

The 25th Amendment of the Constitution, ratified in 1967, details the order of succession that we use today should our president die, resign, be impeached, or become otherwise unable to fulfill the duties of the office. Prior legislation had addressed this issue, but this amendment also dictates procedures to be used should something happen to the vice president. Prior to this amendment there was no provision to replace the vice president if the vice president died, left office, or became president—the office simply remained vacant. When President Kennedy was assassinated in 1963, Lyndon Johnson, then vice president, assumed the presidency having already had a heart attack. This situation provided cause to reassess the succession for the president and vice president. According to the 25th Amendment, if we lose our vice president, the president would nominate a person (who may or may not be noted in the list below) to become the vice president and take office upon confirmation by a majority vote of both houses of Congress.

Listed below are the first six positions in the order of succession should the president die or leave office:

1. Vice President
2. Speaker of the House of Representatives
3. President Pro Tempore of the Senate
4. Secretary of State
5. Secretary of the Treasury
6. Secretary of Defense

For more information about the 25th Amendment, visit http://case law.lp.findlaw.com/data/constitution/amendment25.

What does the term *third world* mean?

We often hear the term *third world country*. It was first used in 1952 by a French economist, Alfred Sauvy, to classify all countries not aligned with NATO or the USSR. It is now typically used to identify countries considered by the West as underdeveloped economically, socially, or in other ways. These often include certain African, Asian, or Latin American countries. Less heard are the cold war terms *first world* and *second world*. *First world* applies to the democratic West, which includes the United States, Canada, Western Europe, Japan, Australia, and New Zealand. *Second world* applies to the Warsaw Pact nations, such as the former Soviet Union and certain eastern European and Asian countries. Many politicians and anthropologists consider these "world" designations to be artificial, outdated, unfair, and even insulting in some regards, especially as it is the *first world* nations often making the judgments as to which countries fall into the given categories.

Despite the reticence of many to use this terminology, it is still widely used. In fact, the term *fourth world* came into use, albeit limited, in the 1970s to describe cultural or ethnic groups or indigenous peoples that preceded existing national boundaries. This would include the Native Americans of North America and the Aborigines of Australia.

What are petroglyphs?

Petroglyphs are images that are carved, abraded, or etched into a rock surface. They date back to 10,000 to 12,000 BC, carved by prehistoric peoples, notably during the Neolithic period. They are still created today by some primitive cultures. It is believed that petroglyphs were originally created for religious, communication, and/or artistic purposes. They should not be confused with pictographs, which are images painted on rocks.

The word *petroglyph* comes from the Greek *petros* (stone) and *glyphein* (to carve). Petroglyphs can be found throughout the world—notably in Africa, Siberia, Scandinavia, Australia, and the southwestern United States.

What are ramparts?

Ramparts are typically associated with forts or other fortified places. They are broad, earth-filled walls, or may be simply earthen embankments. The purpose of a rampart is to protect the inner workings or buildings of the fort from enemy fire. Most Americans are familiar with the word *ramparts* as part of the nation anthem, "The Star Spangled Banner." It begins,

> O say, can you see, by the dawn's early light,
> What so proudly we hail'd at the twilight's last gleaming?
> Whose broad stripes and bright stars, thro' the perilous fight,
> O'er the **ramparts** we watch'd, were so gallantly streaming?

Now a national monument, Fort McHenry (near Baltimore, Maryland) was the site of the 1814 Battle of Baltimore, a key operation in the War of 1812. Because of its strategic location, Major George Armistead, commander of Fort McHenry, anticipated a strike. He ordered that a flag be made much larger than was customary so "the British will have no difficulty in seeing it from a distance." In the meantime, Francis Scott Key, a 35-year-old Maryland lawyer, learned that a friend, Dr. Beanes, had been captured by the British purportedly for anti-British activities. Key, accompanied by Col. John Skinner, a government prisoner of war exchange agent, located the British fleet in the Chesapeake Bay, where they successfully negotiated Beanes's release. However, having heard far too much information regarding the impending attack on Fort McHenry, the three men were detained for security reasons until the battle concluded. It is from one of these ships that Key was able to observe the siege. The fighting concluded in the wee hours of the morning of September 14. With no natural lighting or illumination from the artillery, Key had to anxiously await the morning to see whose flag could be seen over the ramparts of the fort. Upon seeing the American flag, Key was so inspired that he began penning the now famous words to our national anthem.

"The Star Spangled Banner" became the official national anthem in 1931 by an act of Congress. The original flag that flew over Fort McHenry now hangs in the Smithsonian Institution. It is now customary to ceremonially fly the first issue of a new flag at Fort McHenry (for example, the first 49-star and first 50-star flag were flown there first), where they remain on protective display after being lowered from the flagpole.

Why is New York City called the *Big Apple*?

As with many things, several accounts exist regarding the origin of New York City's nickname. According to the Society for New York History, the word *apple*, in addition to that of the fruit, had another meaning or connotation in the 1800s. "Apple" often referred to a variety of illegal, unsavory, or disreputable temptations generally thought or known to be conducted in New York. To counter this trend, the Apple Marketing Board mounted a vigorous advertising campaign to restore a more positive image to the word, particularly by promoting the use of phrases such as "American as apple pie."

In 1909 Edward S. Martin in *The Wayfarer of New York* lamented that New York got more than its fair share of the nation's wealth and likened the city to the fruit of a tree when he said, "The big apple gets a disproportionate share of the national sap." However, according to Barry Popik, a New York City slang historian, it was in 1924, thanks to horse-racing columnist John J. FitzGerald, that "Big Apple" became truly associated with New York City. While on assignment, FitzGerald reportedly overheard stablehands in New Orleans using "big apple" to refer to their goal of racing in New York. He liked the nickname and used the phrase to name his column "Around the Big Apple" in the *New York Morning Telegraph*. In fact, the New York City Council later named the intersection of West 54th Street and Broadway, where FitzGerald lived, "The Big Apple Corner" in his honor!

"The Big Apple" achieved even more popularity during the 1930s and 1940s when used by jazz musicians as a term for "the good life," success, or realizing a dream—to play *the Big Apple*! Its use faded until the early 1970s, when the New York Convention and Visitor's Bureau initiated an active campaign to encourage tourists to visit New York—*the Big Apple*. The city's nickname stuck and is now used and recognized nationally and internationally.

What is flag etiquette?

The flag is a symbol of national pride. Senator Henry Cabot Lodge (1850–1924) aptly stated: "The flag stands for all that we hold dear—freedom, democracy, government of the people, by the people, and for the people." Because the flag is used for a variety of civilian purposes, by individuals and organizations, the need arose to define how the flag should be respectfully displayed and handled. The United States Flag Code was authored in 1923 as a guide for the flag's use, display, and care. It was amended in later years. The military does not follow this flag code because each branch has its own code regarding proper flag etiquette.

Some guidelines from the U.S. Flag Code are:

- When a flag is displayed as a lapel pin, it should be worn on the left lapel—near the heart.
- When the flag is displayed on a wall, it should be displayed with the union (the blue field with stars) uppermost and to the observer's left.
- The flag, when it is in such a condition that it is no longer a fitting emblem for display, should be destroyed in a dignified way, preferably by burning.

These are but a few of the guidelines in the flag code. For more complete information about flag etiquette, visit www.legion.org or www.vfw.com.

Are there standard criteria used to designate bodies of flowing water such as rivers, creeks, or streams?

Put simply—no. In the United States, according the U.S. Department of the Interior (www.doi.gov), many geographical terms such as *river*, *creek*, *pond*, and *lake* have no set definitions or their definitions are so broad that they are of no use. The same is true of land terms such as *mountain* or *hill*. Different states or organizations responsible for naming geographical features are highly susceptible to individual perception. For example, most would agree that a stream is smaller than a river or that a pond is smaller than a lake;

however, there are many exceptions to this in naming bodies of water in the United States, as noted in the federal government's maps and databases.

The Department of the Interior classifies all "linear flowing bodies of water" as a stream, yet there are 121 generic terms that fall within this rather broad designation. Many governmental entities and individuals would insist that a stream is a flowing body of water that flows into a river, yet there are exceptions to this rule of thumb, too. The government has made numerous attempts over time to create specific definitions simply to reduce confusion and to create some logical degree of order, but these efforts have been abandoned along the way due to cultural, historical, or sentimental reasons and/or mistaken designations at the time of the waterway's finding or mapping.

Credits and Resources

Topic ideas were provided by readers as follows:

Robert Ambrose: posh
Paul and Judy Bagnall: bees and honey
Roger Beitel: cartographer
Butch Bellas: bison (eastern woodlands); squared away; flat/apartment
Elizabeth Campbell: up to snuff
Patti Campbell: cold turkey; rank and file; Sudoku
Aly Codrick: pink flamingo
Covenant Presbyterian Preschool Board: biannual/biennial
Cathy Cummings: sleep tight
Becky Dempsey: field trip; leaf burning; diabetes; p's and q's; jacks (along with the fourth-grade class at Valley School); nip it in the bud; meaning of Christmas; billiards/pool; surname suffix; cousins; Dutch oven
Bill Dempsey: mushroom
Linda Flickinger: daylight saving time
Lillian Graber: Groundhog Day
Roberta Graham: Coudersport Ice Mine
Heitzer family: medicine ball
Ben Helterbran: Hoosier
Buddy Helterbran: uvula
Joyce Henderson: mahimahi
William Higgins: yin and yang; oyster crackers

Credits and Resources

Sally Iscrupe: outhouse

Monica Ivory: over-the-counter

Jo-Anne Kerr: homing pigeon

Kelli Jo Kerry-Moran, PhD: pretzel

Tim Komar: bee sting

Arlene Lowry: eyeteeth

Jack McCracken: standard criteria

Angela McDonnell: flag etiquette

Mona McKee: benchmarks

Leslie Nemeth: anti-Semitism

Linda O'Sullivan: humans on Mars; governmental summit

Linda Perry: insects as pests; fog

Shelly Picard: wreck of the *Hesperus*

Connie Pilz: plastic recycling

Rachel Roehrig: St. Nicholas/Santa Claus

Jennifer Rotigel, EdD: cats purring; maître d'

Cassie Rummel: slow as molasses

Lisa Sajna: flammable/inflammable

Rick Schwab: catch-22; Easter (date set); prothonotary; Yogi Berra; New Hampshire's motto

Judy Shomo: cat's meow

Geraldine Torrence: buttons

Marty Treasure: summer and winter; Donner Pass

Lori Von Stein's fourth-grade class at Holy Trinity School: school; computer

Blanche Clarke Weitershausen: gobbledygook; chip off the old block; limeys/blokes; London broil; A.Q.; pitted ham

Vernie West: vision; apple of my eye; scapegoat; nimrod; salary

Steven Williams: Neapolitan ice cream

Consultants

Lt. Col. Jerome Ashman, USAF (Ret.): heat lightning; Mars

Drew Banas: standard criteria

Tom Clendaniel: tessellations; topology

Anne Coyne, RPh: over-the-counter

Rev. Robert D. Cummings: Hogmanay

Chef William Hunt, CEC, CCE, AAC: sous chef; pitted ham

Ellen Keefe: plastic recycling

Kaitlin Nemeth: Hanukkah

Leslie Nemeth: anti-Semitism

Randall C. Orndorff: benchmarks

Cindy Shaffer: computers

Tom Tatone: vegan

Mark Von Stein, RN, MN, CCRN: blood pressure

Resources

American Heritage Dictionary of the English Language (4th edition)

The American Mushroom Institute

Merriam-Webster Dictionary

National Audubon Field Guide to North American Insects and Spiders

PADI Open Water Diver Manual

Pennsylvania Department of Conservation and Natural Resources (DCNR)

Roget's II: The New Thesaurus (3rd edition)

Webster's New World College Dictionary

Internet sites are noted within the text of selected topics.

Photo Credits

Jennifer Rotigel, EdD: flamingo

Richard and Faith Russell: Halloween

Rick Schwab: bison. Photographed on the University of Buffalo campus; bronze reproduction of an original by G. H. Messmore, sculptor.

Helen Sitler, PhD: purring; cat's meow

Valeri R. Helterbran: all other images

Trademark Acknowledgments

Hefty is a trademark of Pactiv Corporation.
Jake Brake is a trademark of Jacobs Vehicle Systems, Inc.
Salada Tea is a trademark of Redco Foods, Inc.

Index

Index

Opportunity to Interact

Readers often contact me with intriguing topics or
topic questions to research.
Do you have one?
Contact me at helterbran@comcast.net if you do!
If your topic question is chosen for use in future publications, you
will be credited as the contributor.
Thank you!
Valeri R. Helterbran

About the Author

Valeri R. Helterbran, educator and author, is an associate professor in the Professional Studies in Education Department at Indiana University of Pennsylvania in Indiana, Pennsylvania. She teaches undergraduate and graduate courses in pedagogy, curriculum and instruction, and leadership studies. Helterbran is a lifelong educator who has taught at the elementary and secondary levels. In addition, she was a middle school and high school principal for almost two decades. She holds a doctorate in educational leadership from Duquesne University, a master of education and a educational specialist degree from the College of William and Mary, and a BA in biology from Randolph-Macon College. She was named as 2005 Pennsylvania Teacher Educator of the Year by the Pennsylvania Association of College and Teacher Educators.

Helterbran often gives presentations, seminars, and workshops on such topics as Socratic seminaring, professionalism, character education, lifelong learning, and professional development for educators and writes scholarly and practitioner articles on these and other educative topics.

In 2007 Helterbran coauthored *Planning for Learning: Collaborative Approaches to Lesson Design and Review.* She also writes a weekly column in her local newspaper, the *Ligonier Echo,* called "Things Every Kid Should Know."

She also loves pugs, traveling, and scuba diving.